WE ARE WANDERERS WE ARE SEEKERS

A Bergthold Family History

GARY D. BERGTHOLD

FriesenPress

One Printers Way
Altona, MB R0G 0B0
Canada

www.friesenpress.com

ISBN
978-1-03-918544-9 (Hardcover)
978-1-03-918543-2 (Paperback)
978-1-03-918545-6 (eBook)

1. REFERENCE, GENEALOGY & HERALDRY

Distributed to the trade by The Ingram Book Company

WE ARE
WANDERERS

WE ARE
SEEKERS

PREFACE

We are wanderers.

We are seekers.

The Bergtholds have always been travelers. This book is about travel as discovery—a journey across five centuries and eighteen generations. Our family traveled from Switzerland to France to Germany to Ukraine and Russia. Some stayed along the way, but most finally found refuge in America, fanning out from Minnesota to all corners of the country.

This is the story of their search for freedom and prosperity, but more deeply, it's the story of how we became ourselves. This is about our genealogy, the history of our genes. Our building blocks. Genealogy is also the story of decisions and serendipity:

- If Great-Grandpa Heinrich had not fled the conflicts of the Kuban settlement and brought the Bergthold family to America …

- If my maternal grandfather, Gus Liesch, had not gone to work that day threshing wheat near Mountain Lake …

- If young Mary Ebert had not cooked the *borscht* and brought it to the hungry workers and had not smiled at the handsome, dirty-faced stranger …

- If my father, Glenn, had not inherited a beautiful tenor voice and traveled to Reedley to sing in a men's chorus …

- If beautiful eighteen-year-old Viola had not decided to travel with friends to the Mennonite conference and been dazzled by Glenn's flashing white teeth and huge smile …

I would not be here.

Or perhaps we aren't an accident. Isaiah 44:2a says, "*I am your Creator. You were in my care even before you were born.*" This story is not only about the makeup of our DNA but also about who we are in a deeper sense. We can't choose our genes, but we can choose our values and beliefs. What I have learned in my research has helped me understand how the early travelers in my family shaped our values and our ideas. The choices we make now will determine which of those values we will pass to the next generations.

HOW I BECAME INTERESTED IN
BERGTHOLD FAMILY HISTORY

I am Daniel Bergthold's great-great-great-great-great-grandson and the great-grandson of Heinrich. Daniel and Heinrich took great risks by moving their families to strange new lands, and as a result, my children and I have opportunities and freedoms about which they could only have dreamed.

I became interested in our family history a number of years ago while attending a family reunion. It was the food that got me started. It's always about food in our family! Armies travel on their stomachs and so do families. *Arabus, borscht* and *varenike* were my favorite foods as a child. They were my family's soul food. The stories told by my many uncles and aunts were well-worn tales of growing up in a large and very poor family that laughed in the face of every hardship. Many of the family jokes included these words for food, and the very mention of them brought peals of laughter from the older generation. I assumed that these words were derived from our German-speaking past, but in visits to Germany, I could never find *varenike or borscht* on the menu.

What started my investigation of our family roots occurred in Ukraine. I had just arrived in Lviv, Ukraine in 1995 to train Ukrainian doctors in improved clinical teaching techniques. Seated in a dark basement lunchroom in a dilapidated maternity hospital in Lviv, my doctor-participants were speaking in Russian and Ukrainian, languages I did not understand. I was tired from the long trip from California and a morning speaking in short sentences so my words could be translated. Being in a group that is speaking a language you do not understand gives you total privacy and freedom to think your own thoughts. I sometimes laughed with the group at what I supposed was a joke. It was a way to seem less lost than I really was.

I was hungry and the smell of the food cooking over a wood fire in the kitchen seemed strangely familiar and comforting. The waiting lunch crowd grew suddenly quiet when the elderly cooks emerged from the dark kitchen with steaming pots. I heard my participants ask questions of the cook, and although I did not understand what they were saying, I recognized two words – *varenike* and *borscht*. Excited thoughts began to race in my mind. These were the foods of my childhood. Not the red beet borscht of Russian restaurants, but the dill and green cabbage soup my mother and grandmother had served. The meal was followed by a tray piled high with watermelon. I pointed at the tray and asked "*Arabus*?" "*Da*," they replied. "That's what it is called in the Russian language." I realized right then that my family may not have originated in Germany, but possibly in Ukraine or Russia. I could not wait to find out more.

The very next day I began my search for the ancestral home of the Bergtholds. The process of learning about our family history has been amazing. Most of the history was forgotten as the family became more American, secular, and affluent. My parents' generation knew very little about this history, as their parents didn't pass it on. Perhaps it was an effort to avoid the stigma of being German during the war, as well as the process of becoming American that is experienced by many recent immigrants. Much of what I learned over the next few years I obtained on the Internet through contacts I made. I've often wondered what old Daniel would have thought about that! It took him months to receive a letter telling of opportunities in Galicia.[1]

Discovering the history of Daniel and the other ancestors, and visiting their land, brings them back to life in our memory. I hope this story helps my children, grandchildren, and their cousins to understand and appreciate their very special past.

CHAPTER ONE

THE SWITZERLAND ROOTS

My first experience in Ukraine only piqued my interest about where the Bergthold family started and where they lived in those times. It was a giant puzzle, and I was determined to put together all the pieces. I assumed that the Bergtholds lived in Ukraine for some time because of the language similarities I had discovered, but how did they get there? As I did more research, I realized that the Bergtholds, who were farmers and Anabaptists (or "Taufers"), would have originated in Switzerland, because they were undoubtedly part of the Anabaptist presence there in the 1500s. The Anabaptist movement against the State Church of Switzerland was a widespread revolt and had developed as a result of Martin Luther's rebellion against the Catholic Church.

When a young Catholic monk named Martin Luther broke with the Church of Rome over doctrinal and political issues on January 21, 1525, the Protestant movement began to spread all over Europe. Part of this movement, called Anabaptism, swept through the Germanic portion of Switzerland. The price of becoming an Anabaptist was high. Prison, fines, torture, and even death faced those who were bold enough to join the movement.

The Reformation swept up the Rhine into Germany from its Swiss source and eventually reached the Netherlands. There a young Catholic priest named Menno Simons, troubled by excesses in State Church practices and doctrine, broke with the Church in 1536 and became an Anabaptist. His followers and my ancestors eventually became known as Mennonites. Their key religious beliefs included adult baptism of believers, a deep sense of community for meeting social needs, a strong commitment to peace and pacifism, and the importance of a personal relationship with God.[2]

Knowing about the prevalence of Anabaptists in Switzerland in the years after Martin Luther prompted me to continue looking there. We were farmers but also wanderers and seekers. While reading some history of the Mennonites, I was able to trace their origins to the so-called Swiss Brethren, an Anabaptist group that formed near Zürich in the face of imminent persecution for their rejection of the demands of the Zürich reformer Huldrych Zwingli. Many decades of persecution by the Catholic Church and the Swiss State Church followed, driving these groups to move to other countries. Our ancestors traveled because they had to in order to survive. It turns out the earliest mention we can find of the family name is in Switzerland. Variations of the name (Bechtold, Bergtholdt, etc.) may possibly date us back to the Middle Ages and the Dukes Berchtold I to V, although I don't have definitive evidence of that relationship.[3]

I decided to visit Switzerland on one of my work trips and find out more. I started with the Emmenthal area because of its rich farmland. Surely there had been Bergtholds there, because of their farming traditions. As part of my research in Switzerland, I visited the Emmenthal Valley several times. If the Bergtholds did come from Canton Bern, the Swiss people of the Emmenthal Valley may have protected the Anabaptists from persecution, because the Swiss were also very independent. In the Emmenthal they may not have been landowners (and therefore left few records), because many lived "underground" to avoid detection from the authorities. The more I learned about the Emmenthal Valley, the more I became persuaded that we could well have lived there long ago. It felt like home to me.

The town of Lutzelfluh in the Emmenthal Valley

As with so much research like this, the historical information provided me with the opportunity to invite my brother Jack, my brother Roger and his wife, Dona, and my cousin Gordy and his wife, Elizabeth, to join my wife Linda and me for a few weeks' vacation in a farmhouse we had rented near the town of Lutzelfluh in the Emmenthal Valley. There we could find out more about the Bergtholds and have a fun vacation at the same time.

The night they all arrived, we started with yodeling. Why? Bergtholds love to sing. They were undoubtedly great yodelers. While we were staying on the farm, we learned more about what yodeling really is. It's not "ohdelay-y-oh." It's beautiful a cappella choir singing. Before they arrived, Linda and I had arranged for a surprise. It was toward dusk, and everyone was feeling jet lag and wanted to go to bed. Dona looked out of the house and said, "Who are all these people walking up the road in costumes?" Suddenly, we heard the most heavenly sound accompanied by the tinkling bells of Swiss cows, who were curious about what was going on. It was a yodeling choir. To the surprise of the choir, Gordy, who had the most experience and vocal expertise among us, quickly joined in. We had an evening of impromptu singing, scatting, and drinking. The low point of the evening was when they asked all of us to sing, and the rest of us could only come up with a pathetic "I've been working on the railroad," sung slightly off key. Who cared? Those singing genes did not transfer to everyone!

The yodeling choir at the Roethlisberger farm

I found many small cultural clues that the Bergtholds may have lived in Switzerland. The family that hosted us in the Emmenthal, Christian and Verena Roethlisberger, told us of a common Swiss poem shared with children that was identical to what my Grandpa Jake used to recite to us in California: "*Ride, ride, rushkin, globen staten schluskin*." And our family love of cows, gardening, farming, and even yodeling seemed perfectly consistent with everything we experienced on that trip. Even the food was familiar to us—sauerkraut, sausage, and *rosti*, a Swiss version of hash browns. As Bergtholds, we found many variations on our name everywhere we went, but almost no one had trouble pronouncing our version.

As I delved further into the history of potential Bergtholds in Switzerland, I learned of a Swiss historian named Professor Hanspeter Jecker, who had published a book on the early history of the Anabaptists in Switzerland. Variations on the name Bergthold were featured prominently in his book. He noted, "In the second half of the seventeenth century, representatives of the Berchtold family played an outstanding and pivotal role in the history of Anabaptism in Basel."[4] Aha! I now had even stronger evidence that the Bergtholds were from Switzerland, but probably not just the Emmenthal. Some of our ancestors most likely lived in the area of Switzerland near the border of Alsace in the Basel area.

Left to right: Roger, Jack, Gary, and Gordy Bergthold in Switzerland in 2000

Who were these Bergtholds, and were some of them our direct ancestors? As Anabaptists, their names may not have ended up in State archives, as these were mostly kept by the established Church. Also, we don't know the exact spelling of the name Bergthold. Names changed spelling from place to place, and spelling was inconsistent from document to document. We believe that the name was spelled "Bergthold" when the family finally emigrated to America in 1877.[5] How many times had the spelling changed before that? We don't know. Such is the challenge of studying family history.

One of the most common variations on our name seemed to be "Berchtold." In fact, there are Berchtolds still living in Switzerland. This may be the spelling that phonetically is most similar to Bergthold in the Swiss dialect of German called *Schweitzer Deutsch*. Other spellings I've come across on the Internet are Bergtholdt, Bergdoll, Bergdolt, Bergtholpt, Bergdold, and Bergdodt.[6]

Despite the confusion over the spelling of our name, I thought there might be a strong link between the way we spell Bergthold now and the many references to Anabaptists called Berchtold. The name Berchtold still shows up in towns like Aesch, near Basel, and in the Canton of Solothurn, also in northwestern Switzerland.

When we visited the Emmenthal, I had a breakthrough. As happens in this type of research, walls break down suddenly and unexpectedly. I had sent an email to Jean-Jacques Bergdolt of Alsace (the German-speaking province of France near Switzerland), whose website I had seen. He replied that his ancestors were *Berchtolds* and came from a place called Schmiedrued in the Canton of Argovia (now called Aargau), also in the northwest of Switzerland. Schmiedrued (which means "blacksmith's grave") is in the region of Lenzburg, between Zurich and Basel. The dates on Jean-Jacque's ancestors' move to Alsace from Switzerland were about the same as the time I believed our ancestors may have left Switzerland for Alsace as well. Many Swiss

Anabaptists fled to Alsace as well as Germany in those days because of the intense persecution by the Church and the State in Switzerland. [7] [8]

No trait is more useful to the seeker than boldness and curiosity. Information in the Jecker book about a winery called the Klushof suggested a Peter Berchtold was the owner at one time. Berchtolds apparently not only liked to farm and eat; they enjoyed wine as well.

I was determined to learn more about the Klushof area during my next trip to Switzerland. One morning I drove to Thurnen, ten miles from the Klushof and where I had discovered that Peter Berchtold had been born. Thurnen is a small suburban town with few signs of seventeenth-century life. I found a short history of the town at the post office and was working to translate it when a young, disheveled man walked by. "*Sprechen Sie English?*" I said.

"Yes, I was born in Santa Monica," he replied. "My parents were students at UCLA!"

My new friend, Tony, proceeded to translate the town history into English for me: "Thurnen is built on both sides of the river, in the entry of the valley. It was a Roman town in 1100 and was called 'Durnum.' In the eleventh century it was on the main Roman road to Basel. In 1305, Thurnen was owned by the Bishop of Basel. In 1400, the whole valley belonged to Basel, and Basel gave it to the people of Thurnen in 1798. Since 1814 it has been a part of the Sissach Region. Once a classic church existed at Thurnen, but it has been destroyed. Although it's on the train line, Thurnen never had a train station. Thurnen is a farming community and also has other economic activities."[9]

Tony invited me for a cup of coffee and I laid out my story. He got excited about taking me to Sissach to see his "crazy friend" who ran a "Mystery Museum." It was a detour from my mission to explore the winery, but I happily followed. He stopped once to show me the house of General Sutter, the Swiss soldier who built the fort in Sacramento that led to the Gold Rush. A bit further down the road we turned in at a small shop I had noticed earlier. A sign out front advertised "Torture Museum and Tattoo Parlor." Interesting combination!

The crazy guy named Guido Varesi wasn't there, and I prepared to leave, disappointed. Just then, Guido drove up in a black CT Cruiser. He was a small man, dressed all in black. He was eager to show me his collection. I asked him how he became interested in death and torture. He replied that someone gave him toy handcuffs when he was five, and he knew immediately what his life work would be. For most of us, the search for our destiny takes much longer.

The museum is in a small, two-story building that once was, appropriately, a jail. Once inside, my eyes took a while to adjust to the darkness, and I saw before me the most ghoulish collection of death tools: guillotines, stretchers, and screws. The most frightening was the "wheel," on which the hapless were tied after all their bones were broken, and they were forced to die in a public square after three days. Guido explained that these machines were the highest technology of the time and showed the best of Swiss engineering.

Although the Executioner Museum (www.henkermuseum.ch) would be fascinating to almost anyone, my interest was due to the fact that these were the instruments of terror the Church used during the Swiss Inquisition to convince the Anabaptists of the errors of their faith. Peter Berchtold had no doubt observed these things being used, because executions were public events.

The best moment of my visit with the "death angel" was when he asked me my name. He pulled out a book called *Executioners in Bernese Aargau*. The index had eight references to Berchtold. Some of our ancestors were clearly pacifists, but perhaps some were also beheaders. I think we have to choose which genes we will control and which will control us. Maybe it's best to have the entire range of options available should we need them.

Guido wasn't finished, however. He claimed to have studied Medieval German and knew the origin of "Bergthold." It might have two meanings. The first is "pig skinner." The second is "executioner." Was he putting me on? He didn't seem the kidding type, but his entire shtick may have been a put-on. He showed me the Bergthold book and offered me a tattoo. Tony said he was the best tattooist in Switzerland. In the old days, prisoners were tattooed so that they could be easily identified. Guido explained that some erased their tattoos with boiling water, so the tattoos were put on foreheads and cheeks, where boiling water would kill the victim. I considered which tattoo I would choose. I won't divulge my answer.

After my adventure at the Torture Museum that day, I continued driving around Aesch looking for information about the Klushof. Suddenly, I saw a sign that said "Klushof." I turned right and soon was on my way to the vineyard. The Klus is a basin-shaped valley that enables vines to grow under mild climatic conditions. The Romans had recognized the preferential situation and cultivated vines there more than 1,750 years ago.

As I drove toward the buildings of the winery ahead, I spotted a worker wearing a ragged, black t-shirt. He stood up from his task, and on his shirt, I saw the words in English, "You are in the right place." Hundreds of years after Peter Berchtold had purchased the Klushof, the shirt could not have been more accurate.

I parked in front of the large home that faced horse barns and winemaking installations. A lovely woman was walking towards the house and I stopped her. "*Entschuldinsiemich, bitte.* Are you Veronica Koellreuter?" I knew her name from the Klushof website I had found two weeks before. Yes, it was she. "*Ich bin Gary Bergthold aus* America." She repeated the name as though it were familiar. I told her why I was there and asked if she knew of any Berchtolds or Bergtholds who had owned the Klushof long ago. Yes, she said. She had papers and documents. Would I come for dinner at seven so she and her husband could show me the material? I walked around the beautifully-maintained fences of the farm and took pictures of the old buildings, the horses, and the many wine barrels that decorated the property. I walked up a steep hill through gnarly grape vines to get a better view of "our" Klushof. I can't begin to describe the beauty of the place.

It was time for lunch, and my love of Swiss food motivated me to find a little restaurant next to an adjacent winery. I sat down in a courtyard shaded by a giant lindenbaum tree. The waiter handed me the menu, and it took three seconds to decide. I asked for *rosti*, the famous Swiss potato dish. It was more delicious than any I had tasted in the Emmenthal. It had lots of ham, red bell peppers, cheese, and was topped with two perfectly fried eggs. After lunch I walked to the gift shop of the winery and spoke to the shopkeeper. I asked her for the meaning of Klushof. A "klus" is a place where a stream has cut a narrow gorge in a rock. "Hof," of course, means farm. She said there was a klus above the Klushhof, but she hadn't seen it.

Klushof sign

The next day I hiked up to a beautiful spring that is the source of the water that nourishes the grapevines. The valley was beautiful—much like valleys in the Emmenthal and even like our own "klus" valley in Santa Cruz, California.

The Klushof winery

When I got back from my hike, Veronica showed me records that indicated a Peter Berchtold had owned the farm and winery in the sixteenth century. When I was there, I bought *one* vine, and I'm eligible for one bottle of wine per year, if I can ever get there to collect it!

Some years later, Linda and I returned to the Klushof. We ran into Barbara, Veronica Kollreuter's daughter, who was busy preparing for a wedding. She took me to her modern office with state-of-the-art equipment and signed me up for a "Weinstock." She printed the authentication certificate her mother had promised me on her laser printer. It hangs on my wall to this day and says that as a son of Peter Berchtold I am entitled to a grapevine from the Klushof Winery.

CERTIFICATE

This entitles **Gary Bergthold**, Son of Peter Bergthold
Klushof 1540, Adoption of
A Pinot Noir grapevine given at Klushof, Aesch, Basel
From June 5, 2003 to June 5, 2008

Veronica Koellreuter
Aesch, June 5, 2003

Framed certificates of Klushof vine ownership

Barbara went through her papers and shared a variety of items, including some old documents about the sale of the winery.[10] I also got the first installment of five bottles that will come to me as an owner of Klushof stock. Any of my relatives can now visit the Klushof and receive a bottle of wine as they are due!

Gary and Linda in Switzerland 2000

After the first visit to the Klushof, I couldn't shake the feeling that my intention was leading me to even more information about the family. I found that there was paper evidence of a sales agreement regarding the Klushof: "The Bishops' Governor of the Castle of Pfeffingen bestows this extensive property to the beloved Peter Bechtel (later mentioned as Peter Berchtold) and to all his heirs."[11] It mentions that with the Governor's permission, Peter has purchased the Klushof from the previous owner, a miller named Jacob Staeli from Aesch.[12] Considerable quantities of wine were delivered by the Klushof to the Governor and the Bishop during that time. It was still not clear to me which of several Peter Berchtolds was the owner, or even that the original owner was an Anabaptist. But I found that in the mid-1590s, all mortgage payments for the Klushof, previously made in Peter Berchtold's name, were made in the name of his son Michael, who was an Anabaptist.

Michael died in 1618, before the ownership of the Klushof could be resolved. Because it was becoming well-known in the area that the family were Anabaptists, the Governor determined they should not inherit the Klushof upon their father's death. The Governor decided he would like to purchase the Klushof, and it looked like Michael Berchtold's heirs might agree to that. But they had fled to Alsace, to a town called Baldenheim and had sent a letter to the Governor stating that they should inherit the winery. When the Governor heard that, it's reported that he declared, "Tell the sons they could get the money after they prove the rejection of their damned belief and return to the Catholic religion!" [13]

What followed was a struggle over many years between the Governor and the heirs of the Klushof, and the result was never clear enough for me to confirm if there was a repayment to the Berchtolds or not. [14]

There wasn't much movement by the State Church against the Anabaptists in Switzerland from 1580 to 1630. But the *Bauernkrieg* of 1653 changed that. [15] The peasant revolt, although quelled, may have had the effect of encouraging ongoing protests among the citizens. The government in Basel strongly disliked the resistance of the Anabaptists, and the Basel priests complained about the light punishments given to those with rebellious ideas. In 1658, a new priest in Sissach, Daniel Schoenauer, wasn't willing to tolerate the Anabaptists any longer. He ordered the governors of nearby towns to examine the activities of one person whom they considered a dangerous heretic—Peter Berchtold.

On June 25, 1658, Governor Ramsbeck of Homburg reported that Peter Berchtold would not renounce his beliefs. Within two weeks, the authorities in Basel ordered the expulsion of Peter from Switzerland but allowed other members of the church to stay. Within a year, on June 3, 1659, the Governor of Homburg complained again that Berchtold had sneaked back into the country. Peter undoubtedly was hiding across the border in nearby Alsace, where other Anabaptists were living, and traveled back and forth to be with his family. The Governor therefore arrested him and asked for advice about how to proceed. The authority in Basel ordered Peter to be transferred to Basel to be interrogated by the Commission of Seven, a council set up by the Church authorities to investigate and punish heretics. His interrogation was documented in some detail. [16]

Berchtold insisted that he never did anything wrong, but he couldn't leave behind his wife and children, who he said were not Anabaptists and who went regularly to the Swiss church. He said he had no intention of converting them. The discussions with the Commission of Seven showed they thought he was a good person but that he remained convinced of his "erroneous beliefs."

What were these "erroneous beliefs"?

- He did not believe the Old Testament and was reading mainly the New Testament. (The printing press had made the entire Bible available to common people.)

- He did not agree with the Church's teaching of original sin, especially not with the belief that all children are born in sin. Peter said, "Adam's sin has nothing to do with us; we only become sinners when we have our full intellectual faculty and commit sins ourselves."

- As to the question of authority, Berchtold answered that he could only be subjected to civil authority as long as his conscience allowed him to do so. Asked whether he would bear arms, he responded with a decisive "NO" and reminded them that Christ had also ordered Peter to put away his sword in the New Testament.

The Reformed priests of Basel had little hope of changing Berchtold's opinions, especially as Peter had rejected all their offers to teach him the truth. He said that under no circumstances would he belong to the Reformed Church. He believed it was his duty to obey God more than people.

As a result of his defiance, Berchtold was ordered to be expelled again, with the threat of death if he should disobey. His wife and children had to remain in Switzerland and be observed by the authorities. His wife was also interrogated, but when she was asked about the erroneous beliefs of her husband, she responded that she would let God judge. She was only responsible for her own beliefs, she said. She begged to be allowed to leave with Peter, but the priests talked her into staying.

Two years later, in 1661, the priest of Sissach informed the authorities that Berchtold had been seen again in the area. He was arrested but let go again. Fortunately, there had been some rule changes that allowed his family to stay, and some new orders that required strict adherence to the expulsion of non-believers, so Berchtold was never jailed or killed. When Peter was banished in 1658 and went to Alsace, the Bishop took over the Klushof. Eventually, the rest of Berchtold's family joined him in Alsace to live and work.

I am in awe of Peter's courage when he was questioned on his Anabaptist beliefs. I'm thankful that he was able to choose banishment over the torture of the wheel. We are indeed survivors. We come from strong roots.

CHAPTER TWO

ESCAPING TO ALSACE

I now needed to understand more about why and where Peter Berchtold and so many other Anabaptists fled when they left Switzerland. Some went directly to Germany, but from the book of Professor Jecker, I had learned that Peter Berchtold and his heirs went to an area in Alsace called Baldenheim, a short distance from St-Marie-aux-Mines (Markirch in German).[17]

Preparing for a visit to the area with Linda in 2003, I emailed Professor Jecker to confirm the presence of the Peter Berchtold family in Alsace and to ask for more information about the sale of the Klushof. He replied that Peter Berchtold left the Basel area for good around 1661 or 1662. Peter's official banishment was in 1658, and he probably settled in the Baldenheim area of Alsace. His sons, Fridli and Peter, may have joined him later. Around 1686, his son Peter was reported to be the *Saintleische Meyer* in Baldenheim, which means that he seemed to be the administrator or farmer on a fairly large farm that belonged to or was called *Saintleisch*.[18]

The steep valleys in Alsace were safely out of reach of the Swiss authorities and were relatively easy places to hide. The area was home to mainly silver and lead mining, but the Swiss families found it hospitable for their cattle and farming because of its seclusion and the willingness of authorities to allow the Anabaptists the freedom to live and work in peace.

By the time the Berchtolds reached Baldenheim, they were already part of a group of Anabaptist families who considered Menno Simon to be the leader of their community. Menno Simon was the Dutch priest who gathered the "scattered" Anabaptists of Northern Europe into congregations that were soon called by his name. There were several different groups of Anabaptists during this time: followers of Melchior Hoffman, Thomas Muntzer, Hans Denk, Pilgram, Marpeck, and Jakob Hutter, to name a few. In the Alsace in Markirch and Baldenheim, the Anabaptists who were associated with Menno Simon experienced conflicts with the Swiss Anabaptist leader Jakob Amman. Amman felt the Mennonites were too "worldly," as they wore clothing with buttons.

During my previous visits, I hadn't been able to find the exact Anabaptist location in these areas of the Vosges Mountains, but on this trip with Linda in 2003, we decided to make one more try.

Sainte-Marie-aux-Mines

After a morning coffee and eclairs in Colmar, we drove up the Val D'Argent but found no one who knew where the Anabaptists had lived. We then stopped a solitary old man, Francois, who said in German, "Eight kilometers up the road you will find the Anabaptists." We stopped at an old Swiss-style farmhouse, but the owner knew nothing of the Swiss who had lived here.

After a nap in the car under a shady tree, we drove thirty more kilometers to Baldenheim, a town in the Alsace plains where the Berchtolds had lived. I spotted a lovely country inn where I had eaten before. I always remembered meals I had enjoyed. Lunch was superb, the highlight being the tiny fried fish—*fritures*—and "freedom fries." The French may not be able to win the Tour de France, but they sure know how to make fries.

In Baldenheim we parked near the Town Hall in front of Pierre Bucher's house. Pierre was the man I'd met in 2002 who had given me crucial information on Baldenheim. He emerged into the bright courtyard, blinking from a nap. As he recognized who we were, his mood became jolly. He proceeded to pull out his books and documents, detailing the history of the area. Our conversation was lively but frustrating, as we talked in three languages, each barely understood by one or more of us. While reading some of his documents, Linda noticed that the Bergtholds had lived in a place called Fortelbach. Pierre said it was now called Fertrupt in French and was just outside St. Marie-aux-Mines.

Perhaps as an effort to move from talk to action, he suggested that we go with him to visit the fifteenth-century church eight hundred yards from his home. The church is a history lesson in stone. It was built in 1409 when Baldenheim was prosperous and largely Catholic. Recently discovered frescoes on the inside walls depict the stations of the cross and prominent figures from the Old and New Testaments. Later the Catholic population declined, replaced by Lutherans in the time of Peter Berchtold. The Lutherans painted over the frescoes, which were lost for hundreds of years. Pierre said that the father of Jacob Amman, the Swiss tailor and preacher and founder of the Amish, is buried beneath the floor of the church. When many of the Protestants and the Berchtolds were sent away by Louis XIV, the remaining Protestants and the new Catholics worshiped in that same church, in two sections separated by an iron barrier.

These days the religious conflicts are silent: neither side has prevailed. Only four Lutheran families attend the church, and five Catholic families attend the newer Catholic church that stands next door. European secularism seems to have won. Religion here and in most of Europe has largely lost its hold.

As we walked back to Bucher's house, I felt a kinship and fondness for him that goes beyond a shared interest in genealogy. He showed me his three restored tractors, a Case and two French models. He fired up one of them, a fifties vintage one-cylinder diesel. I myself was a John Deere fan, but we still had a lot in common!

Back to Fertrupt we went. We had passed this place four times on our previous searches but never really noticed it. This time we stopped at a sign announcing "Fertrupt," the town where Mennonites had lived. We were taking a photo when I spotted a woman in the house across the road whose curiosity had gotten the better of her. I beckoned to her, and she came over. Karen was spectacularly helpful. We haltingly explained our purpose, and she got in her car and motioned us to follow.

She stopped at several very old Swiss-looking farmhouses, one which had the date 1591 carved on its door mantel. She explained that these were the houses of the Swiss Anabaptists, large and substantial. Here the exiles from Swiss persecution came, raised cattle, made cheese, and created the most fertile land in the kingdom. They practiced exchange cropping and added fertilizer to the soil, a farming innovation of the time. We've been good at spreading manure ever since.

Karen finally took us to the home of Georges Jung, a retired textile designer whose hobbies include Fertrupian history. Jung, a perfect name for a man who would take me on a journey into my collective unconscious, was busy, but he agreed to talk with us the next morning. As we drove off, Karen looked at our short pants and colorful shirts and joked, "You must not be Amish. They don't come here dressed like that in BMWs."

The next day we kept our appointment with Herr Jung, my "Fertrupt therapist." We learned many interesting things about the Anabaptists who had lived in the area. Georges excitedly bounced between French and German. A blank stare from me would turn him toward Linda and French, until her silence would bounce him back to German. I'm not sure why he worked so hard with us. Perhaps it was our enthusiasm about a subject that interested him as well.

After two hours with Jung, we left Fertrupt for the last time and drove the windy, pine-forested road back over the mountains to the Vin Strasse. I was satisfied that I had finally confirmed the existence of Berchtolds in Alsace, bolstered by the information and documents about the fight between the Berchtold family and the Bishop over the ownership of the Klushof.

It took several trips to finally put in place this piece of the family puzzle. Alsace was the place where Peter Berchtold was involved in the Anabaptist schism, when the Mennonites split from the Amish, and it's probably good that they did or we would all be driving buggies and wearing black fedoras.

Not only did Peter Berchtold's family continue to fight with the Bishop in Basel, but the significant conflict with the followers of Amman over differences in both lifestyle and doctrine accelerated the decision of many Mennonites to leave Alsace for Germany. While they lived in Alsace, the Berchtolds, whom I will now call "Bergtholds," had heard from German friends about opportunities available along the Rhine in Germany. The tensions with the followers of Amman in Alsace were increasing. The Mennonites weren't willing to live under the repressive rules of the Amish and their practice of "shunning," and there didn't seem any way to reach a compromise. A move to the Rhine River in Germany was the next stop on their journey to seek peace and opportunity.

CHAPTER THREE

THE GERMAN CONNECTION

Given the disagreements with the followers of Amman, and the word from other families in Germany that there was opportunity there, a group of Mennonite families who had been living in Alsace packed their belongings, including a few head of Simmental cattle, a pair of pigs, and the *meagrope* (the large cast iron kettle they always took with them), and boarded one of the flat-bottomed rafts that plied the Rhine between Switzerland and the Atlantic. Their destination was said to be Ibersheim, a small village on the banks of the Rhine River five miles downstream from Worms. After floating down the slow-moving river for a day, the families changed rafts and walked to another raft at the bottom of the falls. From there the trip took them two days.

My research had identified that I was directly related to a Daniel Bergthold, married to Marie Lichti in Harxheim, a town not far from Ibersheim. Daniel ran the family vinegar distillery. I don't know exactly when Bergtholds arrived in the Pfalz. I only know that there are descendants of Daniel Bergthold who live in Ibersheim to this very day.

Ibersheim and Harxheim were the foothold of the early Mennonites in the Pfalz (called the Palatinate), a small kingdom ruled by a Protestant prince named Karl Ludwig. Europe at the time was composed of many warring kingdoms.

Adam Giesinger[19] writes:

> Germany in the eighteenth century was a crazy quilt of more than three hundred states, more or less independent, ranging in size from a few acres to large and powerful nations like Austria and Prussia. In theory, all were part of the Holy Roman Empire, ruled over by the Emperor, who was chosen for life by the Electors, the leading Princes of the Empire. In practice, the power of the Emperor was a fiction. By custom the title had become hereditary in the House of Hapsburg, the rulers of Austria, who ruled not only Austria within the Empire but also large areas outside inhabited by Hungarians and Slavs. The Emperor's authority over the German Princes was largely ignored by these, his nominal subjects. Every little prince, even if he ruled only a few square miles, was a law unto himself; the greater princes were independent sovereigns, who did not hesitate to make war even on the Emperor himself.

Religious differences and the lack of religious toleration embittered the life of the people. In the Middle Ages there had been religious unity in Germany and with it a semblance of political unity under the Emperor. Martin Luther's quarrel with the Papacy had split the country into warring parts, which no Holy Roman Emperor was ever able to weld together again. There followed a century of religious war, with the Catholic Emperor on the one side and the Protestant North German Princes, often assisted by foreign powers, on the other. After indescribable devastation and decimation of the population, the series of wars was ended in 1648 by the Peace of Westphalia.

The turmoil and frequent wars in Germany must have had devastating consequences on the Bergthold family, which had settled with other Mennonites in the German Palatinate, hoping for a more peaceful life. According to the *Mennonite Encyclopedia*,[20] Daniel Bergthold's father was Jakob Bergthold, and his grandparents and great-grandparents can be traced back to Peter Berchtold's family in Alsace. There were many Peters, Daniels, and Jakobs in the family all along the way, so it's difficult to pin down exactly who was related to whom. [21] [22]

On one of my trips to that area of Germany, I met an American named Gary Waltner, who was married to a German woman and was the Director of the Mennonite Research Center in Weirhof. During my visit with him, I was able to photocopy documents about Bergtholds who had lived in the area. It motivated me to go to Ibersheim to see if there were any residents there with whom I could speak. My car navigation system took me straight to the old church in Ibersheim. As I stood in front of the church, I looked to the left and saw a sign that said, "DANIEL BERGTHOLDT, SCHREINERMEISTER (Cabinetmaker)."

I couldn't believe my good fortune. I knocked on the gate, which was opened by an older man who said he was Daniel's father. I explained to him in German why I was there. He took me to their house, where I met Daniel and his wife, Annette, and baby boy.

To my surprise, Daniel spoke perfect, unaccented English. He had spent several months in Reedley, California but hadn't met any of the many Bergtholds living there. Over a typical and tasty German lunch of sausage and sauerkraut, Daniel told me that many Bergtholds were still living in the Pfalz, and his story of the Bergthold family in that area was consistent with the research I had done. We exchanged emails, and I promised I would return. It was an emotional day for me, because I never thought I would actually find any Bergtholds still living there. As I drove out of the compound that day, the car radio was playing "Amazing Grace," which brought me to tears and caused me to pull over, as I thought again about the role of intention in finding lost family ties.

Daniel Bergtholdt in Ibersheim

Daniel and Annette in Ibersheim

During the time the Bergtholds lived in Germany, Prince Karl Ludwig invited the Swiss Mennonites to lease the devastated and depopulated lands that had been confiscated from the Catholic Church and were now in the hands of the Protestant princes. The Mennonites had been primarily dairy farmers in Switzerland and Alsace, but they distinguished themselves in the Palatinate as pioneers of progressive agriculture, techniques they had perfected in Alsace. In addition to crop rotation, they introduced the use of clover and feedlot practices and the growing of potatoes, which only a few years earlier had been imported from South America.

In short, they practiced farming methods that were not in general use in Germany at the time, and they became known as "the master farmers of Germany." The Mennonite farmers were fairly prosperous for a time, but the available land couldn't support the growing population, caused by their practice of having large families. After a few years, some of the Mennonites were again ready to move on in search of new lands and opportunities. There simply wasn't enough land for all those who had settled there.

Professor Peter Bachmann's book, *Mennoniten in Kleinpolen*[23] describes the conditions that prompted the next emigration:

> In the Rhine provinces there was much overpopulation. The four to five yokes
> of land (a "yoke" was 1.42 acres or as much as a yoke of oxen could plow in

one day) were far from enough to furnish a family with a moderate livelihood. And added to that were the frequent war disturbances which ravaged the land. The misery from the latest wars, the intolerant oppressions of the dukes of small states, the selfish actions of their officials, made the homes of the citizens and farmers sorrowful.

A writer at the time said, "Shall we rejoice that for fifty years we were allowed to cultivate our fields by the sweat of our brow, to feed the hogs and rabbits of his highness? Or, shall we rejoice that often we were torn away from our necessary work to build big houses for the high officials? Or that he abandoned us and our laboriously acquired property to a band of ignoble thieves?"

In 1772, Austria took possession of the Polish province of Kleinpolen and named it Galizien (Galicia, a Latin word that means "distant lands" and refers to what is now Western Ukraine). A few months later, Kaiser Franz Joseph II toured the new lands to inspect the economic and political conditions in the area. He found Galicia in "sad condition." Bachmann writes, "Nobility, church officials and monasteries owned large areas. The farmers in the hamlets were poor, stupid and superstitious. Schools were only a few and those few served the nobility. Industrious ventures were nearly unknown in Galicia, and agriculture and forestry were greatly deteriorated." To remedy the situation, Kaiser Joseph decided to colonize the area with German farmers and manual workers, as Polish dukes and kings had done in the Middle Ages. It was not in the Kaiser's interest to call for Austrian immigrants, because the population of Austria had been decimated by the Seven Years' War 1756 to 1763.

At first the immigration of Protestant Evangelicals into Galicia was restricted because of opposition from the Catholic Church. Kaiser Franz Joseph's mother, Maria Theresa, was a strong Catholic and restricted the immigration to non-Evangelical manufacturers and merchants. Farmers were excluded from immigration because of their Evangelical faith. On Maria Theresa's death in 1780, her son became sole ruler, and in 1781 he issued a charter offering Evangelicals great incentives for settling in Galicia. "Every settler should, for ten years, be free of paying interest on land, tax and tribute. He should have a residence and other necessary buildings and 20 to 40 yoke of fields, according to the number of cattle he could acquire with his own means." Settlers were also offered "two oxen or two horses, two cows, two hogs, the necessary tools and implements such as wagons, plows, harrows, good harnesses for horses, axes, hoes, hay and manure forks, scythes, and saws." It was also made known that food was cheap, which was also a strong inducement to immigrate.[24]

The Austrian Kaiser advertised in German newspapers that in Galicia there were large, unoccupied areas that could be homesteaded by the hard-working German farmers. The Kaiser promised the settlers the following:

- Complete religious freedom

- A spacious house and garden for each family

- Good land for fields and meadows, beasts of burden and cattle, and field implements and house furnishings

- Exemption from military duty

- Ten years' exemption from all taxes, tribute, and burden

From what they heard from other German families who had already moved to Galicia, the Bergtholds and other families from Harxheim believed they too could move and create a better life for their families. Thus began the next Bergthold emigration—from Germany to Galicia. Once again, the Bergtholds and other families would pack up their belongings and make the courageous move to another country to find land and peace. The first group of Mennonite families left Harxheim in 1784, and in August 1786, Daniel and Marie and their six children left to join these original six families in Galicia. These weren't easy decisions, and it's likely that Daniel and his family felt substantial ambivalence about the journey ahead.

After my visits to Germany, after a number of memorable meals of *pfalzplatters*—bratwurst, *leberknodel* (liver dumpling), sauerkraut, mashed potatoes, and *spargel* (white asparagus)—I made my way to the next stop on the Bergthold journey: Galicia (Ukraine).

CHAPTER FOUR

THE UKRAINIAN ROOTS

With the departure from Harxheim to Galicia, the next Bergthold emigration had begun. I had traced the family to Ukraine in prior visits, so I now needed to find the villages where the Mennonites had lived. I had read the names of the villages in a book written in German, but I had few other clues as to their exact location. I was looking forward to experiencing the Ukrainian *varenike* I had enjoyed on prior visits, so after a training session with doctors in Lviv had concluded, I finished my lunch and hired a translator and guide, Dr. Andrew Tuziak, to help me search for the villages. Andrew became an invaluable partner in the Galician searches.

Gary enjoying varenike in Lviv

I knew the Mennonite families had lived there from about the early 1780s to the 1820s, and I knew the German names of the villages: Falkenstein, Rosenberg, and Einsiedel (near a

Ukrainian town named Sczerecz). My strategy was to go to the area, stop at a church, and talk to the parish priest about the purpose of my visit. Perhaps the priest would know of the history of these old villages.

Unfortunately, when I got to the church in Sczerecz, the young priest, Father Kohut, didn't know of any German-speaking people who had once lived in the area and could give me no suggestion about where to go next. I stood in silence in the church, wondering if I would ever find someone who remembered our families. It was so long ago.

Gary talking to Father Kohut in the church in Sczerecz

But as we were talking in the church, an old woman suddenly emerged from the shadows of the empty sanctuary and walked slowly towards us. She started out speaking in Ukrainian but then suddenly said—IN GERMAN—"*Rosenberg und Einsiedel.*" Just hearing her say those names gave me a shock. How was it possible she knew the names of those villages now, after so many years?

The woman pointed in the direction of the villages, and the priest then guided me to the places. The little villages were very much like they were in the eighteenth century: the same wells were being used to draw drinking water, and many of the old adobe houses were still in use. Thanks to the research done by Bachmann and many other Mennonites, I had a map of the houses in the villages. In Rosenberg, the original Daniel Bergthold house was still standing and was presently occupied by a Ukrainian "babushka" named Ganna.

Daniel Bergthold's house in Rosenberg with Gary and Ganna

Ganna, the current inhabitant of the original Bergthold house

The house, like the original houses, was built of adobe bricks and wood on a stone foundation. At the end of the village, fifty meters from the Bergthold house, the original schoolhouse also still stands. A communal well in the middle of the road still provides drinking water to the villagers, who say it's the best and sweetest water in the area. Another old woman who lived in the area took me to the well and poured me a drink of water in a symbolic ceremony I shall never forget. I still have a small sample of that water and will keep it forever.

An old woman, Father Kohut, and Gary at the well in Rosenberg

As we sampled the well water, I asked the woman if she knew anything about German-speaking people who had lived there. She did not, and I once again felt the disappointment that often precedes an unexpected discovery. I then asked her, as one of the oldest persons in that village, whether she remembered the Germans. She motioned to a house where an old man named Mr. Vogt lived. I asked her if she would take me to his house. After several sturdy knocks, Vogt answered the door.

Vogt answers the door

Gary interviewing Vogt

He spoke to us in Ukrainian, and my translator, Andrew, explained the purpose of my visit. He seemed confused by my questions about the history of the village. I spoke to him in my few words of German, hoping he would understand what I was looking for. Suddenly, he straightened up and began speaking in German. He surprised himself and commented that it was the first time he had spoken German in many years, but he did remember some German people who had lived there. I told him his German was better than mine, so we continued our awkward conversation. He explained that as a young boy he'd attended the school that had been built by the Germans. I asked him to get into the car so we could identify some of the houses. He refused to ride in the car and started walking down the road with surprising energy.

As we passed each of the old houses, he would say the name of the family who had lived there.

Vogt crossing the road to show the houses where Germans lived

When we returned to his house, I tried to think of what I could give him as thanks for helping me find my family. The only thing I had to offer was the blue LL Bean down jacket I had with me, which looked very different from the heavy, black felt jacket he was wearing. I explained it was made out of goose feathers and would keep him warm in the cold winters. He pointed to all the geese running around, lifted it up and shook it, and laughingly said (translated by Andrew), "This is a piece of shit. It won't even cover my dick." But he took it anyway and said he would give it to his granddaughter.

Gary and Vogt in front of Vogt's house

Vogt examining the LL Bean jacket

On one of my later visits, I brought teachers and students from the school to walk to the village with me, and Vogt came out and told them his stories about fighting the Nazis. I like to think that my visit offered him an opportunity to share his experiences with the local students, who had previously known nothing about him or their history. My connection with Vogt continued until after his death, when his granddaughter asked my translator, Andrew, to send me some mementoes he had asked her to share—an old razor and his medal of honor as a hero of the Soviet Union.

Visiting the villages became a family event when Linda, our son Eric, his wife, Ali, and their young son, Kincaid, came to the villages with us while Eric was working for USAID in Kyiv. As I stood again in front of Daniel's old house with them, I felt a strong connection to the families that had lived there so long ago.

Gary, Eric, and Kincaid in Rosenberg in front of Daniel's house

By the time I found the Galician villages, I had learned a great deal on the Internet from sources like Peter Bachmann and my friend Glen Linscheid about how the Mennonites, including the Bergthold family, had arrived in Galicia so many years ago.

In 1784, three years after the Kaiser's charter was issued, six Mennonite families, all descended from the Swiss Mennonites, had packed their worldly belongings, including the all-important *meagrope*,[25] and bid a tearful farewell to the remaining twenty-one Mennonite families in Harxheim. Two years later, my ancestor Daniel and his wife Marie Lichti Bergthold and their six children joined these original families in the Galician villages. The villages were located about twenty kilometers southwest of Lemberg, the beautiful capital of Galicia, and about three kilometers due west of the town Sczerecz. Sczerecz in the 1780s was a small town of Ukrainian farmers located on a hill topped by a Catholic church that was built in 1410. The church is still standing today, a simple structure with a stone façade and a small steeple. On its white front wall is a plaque that reads in Polish, "Commemorating the Battle of Gruenwald—1410."

The trip to Galicia for the Bergtholds was probably similar to that described by other immigrants to Galicia:[26]

> The families trekked eastward with the wagon on foot in bad weather and
> were on poor roads for days and weeks without shelter. Once they reached
> either Regensburg or Ulm, Bavaria, they boarded riverboats, which took

them as far as Vienna, Austria. In Vienna, all the colonists had to register after a brief stopover. Their trek continued overland by wagon train across the Carpathian Mountains to Lemberg (Lviv) the Capital of Galicia. They suffered many hardships on their long wearisome journey. The rickety wagons rumbled and jolted over dusty, rutted roads in the parching sun. In wet weather they churned laboriously through mud and mire. Sometimes the wagons broke down and makeshift repairs had to be performed for them to continue. Many times their loved ones had to be buried on the roadside without a minister in attendance. Many a mother gave birth to her children under perilous conditions.

Lviv, Ukraine today

Upon their arrival in Lemberg, the Bergtholds and their party had to register again in the office that was set up for implementation of the settlements. "Agricultural authorities were responsible for providing lodging (sometimes with Polish or Ukrainian farmers), building of houses, dividing the land and supplying food until the settlers could make it on their own." [27]

The group of newcomers described the several days they had rested in the beautiful city of Lemberg before walking the last leg of their trip to the villages. They were amazed at the beautiful churches and fortified public buildings they had seen. Lemberg had seen many invasions over the centuries by warring tribes but was now a prosperous trading center perfectly situated between Poland and Russia. Its many churches reflected its stormy history. There were magnificent Russian Orthodox churches, Armenian Orthodox churches, and Catholic churches built by the Poles. Beautiful statues graced every building in the city, and it was said that no one could count the number of lions that were painted and carved in the designs of most buildings. The lion was the symbol of the ruling family of Lemberg. The name of the city was later changed to Lviv, which means "City of Lions" in Ukrainian.

As Daniel and his family crossed the crest of the last hill, they could see their destination—the tiny German villages outside Sczerecz. I imagine that their thoughts went back to their home near the Rhine River in the German Palatinate they had left earlier. Daniel and Marie missed their tiny houses built neatly in a row in the small village of Harxheim bei Heidelberg. They had been married in 1764 when Marie was only fifteen and Dan a young lad of seventeen.[28] Daniel had helped manage a vinegar and wine distillery in Harxheim, where they and other Mennonite families had farmed and maintained beautiful gardens of cabbage, potatoes, carrots, fruit trees, and ever-present pigs. But warfare and threats to their pacifist lifestyle had shattered the orderly, peaceful life they had known. Now on the last leg of their journey, from Lemberg to the villages, their thoughts must have turned to the friends who had preceded them and to the challenge of starting over. Would this new land bring the peace they so longed for?

Letters written back to Germany in the 1780s and cited in Bachmann, described the terrain around the villages as quite level and the land productive. The writer described the native people that the Swiss Mennonites found living in the area: "The Polish (Ukrainian) people are poor. They do not have tables, benches, and beds in their homes. Their clothing is limited and of poor quality. Their appearance is unusual because of large mustaches and odd type of haircut, which consists of one level clip around the head. Their hair has not been touched by a comb."[29]

As the Bergtholds grew closer to the village, they were probably amazed to see that their predecessors had already constructed small houses that were similar in design to those they had left behind. The houses and attached barns were made of mud mixed with straw that was packed tightly into wooden supports and cross beams. The roofs of the houses were made of thatch. Each house had a tiny kitchen and three small rooms. They also saw that, similar to their village in the Pfalz, the houses were facing each other in neat rows separated by a common area about thirty meters wide. In the middle of the common area, a well had been dug to furnish the village with fresh drinking water. Behind each house was a small garden. Already huge cabbage plants were growing, and fruit trees had been planted in neat rows behind each house. Little pigs squealed as they followed their mothers in search of succulent roots.

As the newcomers came within shouting distance, the men, women, and children of one of the villages, Falkenstein, threw down their tools and ran to greet them. Like the newcomers, the residents of Falkenstein were dressed in dark, rough clothing befitting the humble, non-worldly style of their religion. The women wore long dresses and dark, long-sleeved blouses buttoned to the neck. On their heads were white caps. The men wore black baggy pants and loose-fitting shirts covered with wool felt jackets.

After many hugs and shouts of *grossgott* and excited exchanges of information about the events of the past year in Germany and Galicia, the newcomers were invited to what I imagine was their first meal in their new Galician home. The villagers built a fire under the *meagrope* in the communal summer kitchen, a large shed covering a brick oven and stove. Soup was prepared that seemed familiar, but it also had some strange new ingredients. In addition to the familiar potatoes, cabbage, and carrots, it also contained two new ingredients—dill weed and sour cream. The cooks called this new soup *borscht,* a name they had learned from their Ukrainian neighbors, who had taught them how to survive in this new land. Along with the *borscht,* the women prepared delicious ham and *zwieback,* the smell of which brought back instant memories of home.

A modern presentation of traditional borscht

For months, the Bergtholds and their friends had eaten only preserved food, such as sauerkraut, dried zwieback called *ruiskies,* and dried, smoked sausages brought from home. Now, long tables were set outside and the feast began. Lengthy prayers of thanksgiving and old familiar hymns, such as *Gott Ist Die Liebe,* preceded that first feast. Daniel Bergthold, the lay preacher who had been so long awaited, offered the first prayer. It began with the traditional German table grace, one which we still say today:

> *Komm Herr Jesu, sei unser Gast,* Come, Lord Jesus, be our Guest
> *Und segne was Du bescheret hast,* And let this food to us be blessed.

As was the tradition, everyone joined in unison for the end of the prayer, *Gott segne uns* (Amen, God bless us), without which they felt the prayer wouldn't be heard. Daniel's prayer went on to thank God for delivering them from the persecution they had experienced as members of the Mennonite faith.

The welcoming feast in Falkenstein continued. After everyone had eaten the delicious *borscht*, the women brought out the main course—ham accompanied by a strange new dish also learned from the Ukrainian neighbors. This dish consisted of triangular-shaped pieces of dough stuffed with potatoes and cabbage and boiled in water. The Mennonites called this new dish *varenike* and told the newcomers that it was the national dish of Ukraine. Nothing ever tasted so good to the famished visitors as fresh ham and *varenike* covered with ham gravy.

The newcomers noticed that their friends had already picked up a few words in the local language. They referred to their rough houses as *door,* a Ukrainian word that meant rustic or plain. Watermelon, which the Mennonites grew to huge sizes and made into delicious rind pickles, were known by the Russian word *arabus*. (These were the names of food that first persuaded me that my family roots were not German but Ukrainian and Russian.)

The new families knew then that life could be good in this beautiful new land, where cabbage grew to double the size they had seen before, and the Mennonites would be left in peace to worship God in their own way. Before the delicious meal was over, talk turned to plans for building houses and creating a more permanent settlement. Plans had already been made to build houses for the new members of the community. Mennonite traditions called for all members of the community to work together to support any member of the group in need of help.

Man with horse and wagon in Einsiedel, 1997

Field near Einsiedel in 1997

The Bergtholds and the twenty other new families apparently camped near the homes of their brethren in Falkenstein while they built their houses. Three of the families, including the Bergtholds, built their houses in Rosenberg, a newer settlement near Falkenstein and just outside of Sczerecz. Overcrowding in Falkenstein required the establishment of this "sister colony." In 1786, Daniel Bergthold and his wife, Marie, moved into their new house in Rosenberg, called "New Sczerecz" by the Ukrainians. The village had only twelve houses, all facing the road that connected Falkenstein and Szerezc. As described by Peter Bachmann, across the road from Daniel's house was the house of his son Jakob Bergthold.[30]

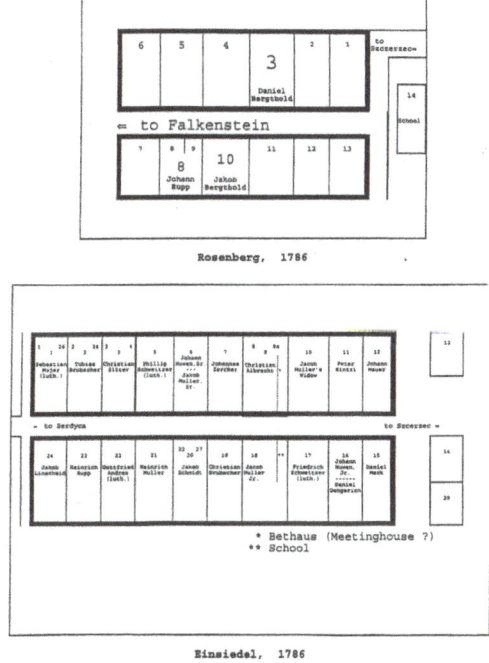

Map of the village homes in Rosenberg

33

Rosenberg was primarily a Lutheran colony, but three Mennonite families, including the Bergtholds, located there. Bachmann speculates that the reason they located in Rosenberg was because it was nearer Sczerecz and sources of employment. A factory had been established there by a wealthy merchant from Lemberg. (On my visit to Sczerecz, I saw several very old brick factories. I imagine the young boys in the Bergthold family may have worked for a time making bricks in these factories to help support their large family and to help construct their home, which had walls of adobe brick.)

I could picture the families breaking the sod with hand implements and marveling at the richness of the sticky, black soil. They probably tasted a bit of the soil to test its fertility, much as I had witnessed my Uncle Victor do on his farm in California. I imagined them laughing at old family jokes, many of them quite earthy, like the jokes that are still a part of my family. I could see the little children playing with homemade stick toys not much different from the toys the children of Ukraine still play with.

Religion was a central part of the life of the villagers. The Mennonites rejected the idea of a permanent clergy and elected one of their elders to perform religious services. Daniel Bergthold was an elected elder and lay pastor of the Mennonite villagers. The original Mennonite church was located in Einsiedel, one of the other German villages.

An old church in Einsiedel

The Mennonite school in Rosenberg

Daniel probably walked or rode horseback between Rosenberg and Einsiedel to deliver Sunday sermons. Sermons at that time were mainly recitations of Bible verses that the elders had committed to memory and discussions of religious themes by the members of the congregation. Music was always an important part of worship. I believe that the beautiful voices of my father, Glenn, the "Singing Bergtholds" of my Uncle Jim Bergthold's children, and my aunts, the Bergthold Sisters, had their roots in the a cappella singing in Rosenberg.

The tiny Protestant villages contained a variety of related sects. Bachmann Joseph Mundlein became the elder minister of several families who formed an Amish congregation. This sect practiced strict adherence to traditional order and discipline and radical separation from the outside world. The Amish Mennonites were known as *Haftlern* because of their rejection of buttons and use of hooks and eyes on their clothing. The Reitish Mennonites were called *Knopflern* because of their use of buttons. Daniel and his family used buttons. Only three of the Einsiedel Mennonites were Amish, and relations between the *Haftlern* and *Knopflern* were apparently good at that point. Intermarriage between the two sects was not infrequent.

Church services were held during the first few years in sheds and crude barns. With the arrival of the new members, the Germans may have decided to build a church. This church would be of a simple design as befitted Mennonite beliefs. It would have no onion-shaped dome as Russian churches, and it would also double as a school for the growing number of children in the village. It was thought to be sinful to travel to church in a wagon, so the church would be built where people could walk to services from the surrounding houses. The Mennonites believed in educating their children well, but the education consisted primarily of religious teaching. It was felt that "new ideas" of science and mathematics were both irrelevant for the life of a farmer and would also lead to "worldliness," a major sin that was to be avoided at all costs.

Several years after the Mennonites settled in Galicia, great news arrived in the villages of Falkenstein, Rosenberg, and Einsiedel. Word of the hard working and prosperous German farmers in Galicia had reached the palace of Kaiser Franz Josef in Vienna. On a trip to the region, he decided to make a personal visit to the villages to see for himself what these enterprising farmers from the west had accomplished. This was a very exciting opportunity, and the village elders met to decide how they could greet the Kaiser and take advantage of the situation. The discussion was long and intense. The Amish members of the community felt that their religious beliefs did not permit cooperation with the civil authorities and certainly did not permit bowing to a Catholic king. The more pragmatic Mennonite members of the community argued that this was an opportunity to secure their land rights and their precious freedom of worship.

The pragmatists won. The great honor of preparing a message for the Kaiser was given to Daniel Bergthold, who besides being the pastor of the humble church was also known as a man who could write beautiful poetry for special occasions, such as Christmas or weddings. Daniel sat down to compose a poem that would both impress the Kaiser and press the colonists' desire to be granted permanent land tenure and religious freedom. Daniel knew that the traditions of the time required flowery and flattering language. It pained him somewhat to write in this style, as it went against the Mennonite traditions of humility and plain speaking. At the end, however, the poem was finished in the flowery style.

A month later the Kaiser arrived with a large entourage and stopped in Einsiedel to view the amazing achievements the Mennonites had accomplished in very few years. The Kaiser and his entourage were seated for a fine meal of ham, *zwieback*, and *varenike*. Several kinds of *varenike* were served, including potato, cabbage, hoop cheese, and fruit. To the delight of his hosts, the Kaiser ate heartily and asked for three helpings of *varenike*. At the end of the meal, Daniel Bergthold arose and from memory recited the following poem in his Swiss-German dialect.

Great, immense are the deeds of
Kaiser Josef

Which he bestows on the Children
of Men.

Oh God, we thank You in that in
Your Grace

You created him for our benefit.

Josef's wisdom has none to
rival it,

Even when one speaks
of Solomon.

In contrast with his equals he

Performs great mercy to others;

As we view Josef's
high intelligence

Then we are near to ecstasy,

Because in close and distant
lands he

Refreshes his people
without prejudice.

Kaiser Josef, I must avow

That I am a Mennonite,

No one of us is looked up to

Though we are still in
Josef's Realm.

We received from Josef the Second

Enough houses, sheds,
and farmland

And care for us as well, and

No less valuable meadows
and pastures.

Even cows, horses, oxen,
and wagon

Are just as large a gift of Grace.

There is verily much to say
of everything.

You gave things of which one
would not even think

Even shovel, hoe, axe, and drill

And many other tools

The Emperor selected for us.

Oh, thanks be to His Majesty!

I am astonished about this,

Almost beside myself with joy!

My tongue sticks to the roof of
my mouth.

We are filled with the wonder of
the things

Which Josef performs for us poor.

Oh, that my thanks should pierce
the clouds

And thank God through
Christ's Blood.

If one traveled through the
whole world

And went through all
man's writings,

He would not find it recorded

In any archive all of what
Josef donates.

When one reads of Alexander,

He would see great things,

And all the deeds that he achieved

To bring the world under him.

Yet no one would show us

Among all of the great deeds

That he had done to all Mankind

What Josef bestows out of
pure kindness.

Josef asks us to believe

And just strongly trust God,

Then good will befall us here.

That's all Josef asks

Of this small bunch
of Mennonites.

But Josef gives us much good also.

Thanks on top of thanks be given
to him

For everything which he does
for us.

As long as we are in this life

Our blood is offered up to him.

Your Majesty, I desire to
give thanks,

Together with my wife and
small children,

Every day of our entire life

Because we are so well pro-
vided for,

For me, my son, and son-in-law.

Yes, we savor these blessings,

Because upon all three of us
has settled

An era that we have prayed for.

Inasmuch as God gives happiness
and health

And blesses our work,

So we have intended

To give continuous tribute.

I would still like to most
humbly submit,

Exalted Majesty,

That no slanderer approaching
with quiet steps

Would be allowed to do
us damage.

With many thanks I would like
to close

And ask His Majesty

When I might enjoy the Grace

Of speaking with His Majesty.

God keep His Majesty healthy for
a long time to come;

May you be continually very
frightening to your enemies.

Through your great military
power may they

All make themselves into
your subjects.

The aforementioned desires to thank and entreat His Royal Imperial Apostolic Majesty. From his all-submissive servant along with my associates. Daniel Bergthold, Mennonite, settler in Neu-Sczerecz (Rosenberg)—July 20, 1786. [31]

At the end of this recitation, the Kaiser arose to thank Daniel for the beautiful words and to thank the village for the fine meal and hospitality. He spoke glowingly of the achievements of the past years and said that it was his hope by inviting the pioneers from the west that their farming techniques and working habits would be adopted by their Ukrainian peasant neighbors. He stated his wish that there be more interaction with the Ukrainian neighbors, but he realized that these Mennonites were a clannish group, whose traditions and beliefs kept them isolated from their non-Mennonite neighbors.

To the villagers' disappointment, the Kaiser made no comment or commitment regarding the subtle and indirect request in Daniel's poem for permanent land tenure and religious freedom. Not knowing whether this omission was a simple oversight or a calculated strategy, they nonetheless couldn't press the issue on such a high official.

After the momentous visit from the Kaiser, the family settled into the normal rhythms of life. In spite of the frontier conditions in which they lived, they tried to duplicate the life they had known in Germany. The days were filled with hard work, and the evenings and Sundays with good conversation and religious observations. One of the highlights of the year was butchering day, which was shared by all members of the community. In the fall, after the crops were harvested, several hogs were butchered and meat was preserved for the long, cold winter. Preparation took days. All the crocks and utensils were scrubbed and the knives sharpened.

On the prescribed day, everyone arrived before dawn. After a hearty four o'clock a.m. breakfast of *grieben* (cracklings) and bread, the men lit the lanterns and went out to slaughter the pigs. The boiling water was taken from the *meagrope,* and the pigs were scalded and the hair removed. Soon afterward the intestines were brought in. The women cleaned the fat off the intestines and cleaned the casings for sausage. Then the cut-up fat was brought in to render for lard and *grieben.* The lard was a prized ingredient for cooking *zwieback* and pies and was used to seal crocks of preserved meat. Salted lard, called *schmaltz,* was also a favorite filling for sandwiches.

The rendering was done in the *meagrope,* which was stirred continually with a wooden paddle by the small boys. After the fat had melted, the ribs were put into the *meagrope* and cooked to a golden brown with the cracklings. By lunchtime the men had cleaned the pig feet and knuckles, and these were placed in crocks with spices and vinegar and sealed to be eaten as pickled meat during the winter. Ground meat, mostly lean trimmings from the hams, was seasoned with salt and pepper and stuffed into the casings for sausage. These were smoked the next day. The next job was stuffing the liver sausage. This was made from one part of liver to four parts meat, mostly trimmings from the neck.

Last but not least came the head cheese. The seasoned mixture of head meat was put into a cloth sack and laid out into a flat pan with a board on top. This board was weighted down with a crock full of cracklings to press out the excess moisture and fat. The next day the head cheese was covered with whey in another stone jar. This would be ready to serve on cold winter evenings accompanied with onions dressed with vinegar. (Most of this butchering and food preparation was continued when the family came to America, and I replicated some of it at my home in Santa Cruz many years later.)

Little is known about Daniel and Marie's later years. Marie died in 1799 at the age of fifty. Daniel died in Rosenberg on February 3, 1806 at the age of fifty-nine and was buried in the Rosenberg cemetery. I was not able to find any trace of his tombstone. During the Soviet occupation of Ukraine, most of the headstones were destroyed, and the marble that had once adorned the headstones was removed. Some of this marble was recycled in the great cemetery in Lviv, where Russian bodies were buried in the graves once occupied by Germans.

We do know that Daniel and Marie had a total of eight children. The youngest two children, Margaretha and Elizabeth, were recorded as having been born in Einsiedel, but most of the family probably stayed in Rosenberg during their lifetime. Either the births occurred in Rosenberg and were recorded in Einsiedel, or Marie went to Einsiedel for childbirth, possibly at the home of a midwife.

Daniel and Marie's first child, Jakob, who was a young man of twenty when the family came to Rosenberg, was baptized in the Mennonite church at Kriegsheim in the Palatinate

four years before the family moved to Galicia. He probably received his religious education in Germany and from his father. He became a well-known preacher, traveling among
the Mennonite colonies and bringing "great joy and love to the faithful," according to the
Mennonite Encyclopedia. Jakob married the younger sister of Jacob Muller, who was the Elder
of the church at Einsiedel.

On December 19, 1787, Jakob was elected preacher and performed that office until 1797.
"On November 3, 1797, Jakob started out on his journey and visited most of the Prussian
churches. Everywhere his bearing and his sermons won him sympathy. All who knew him, says
his obituary, must truly admit that he was an exceptionally faithful and zealous servant of the
Lord, in proclaiming as well as in spreading the saving Word of God." [32]

A major incident is recorded about Jakob Bergthold that must have had a large impact on
the entire family. Two Hutterites from the village of Vishink in the Chernigov province of
Russian Ukraine visited the Galician Mennonites around 1797 to discuss matters of religious
faith with the Amish and Mennonite religious leaders.[33] A year later the two Hutterites again
visited, and soon after that visit, nine Galician Mennonites, led by the lay preacher Jakob
Bergthold, hastily sold their land and moved to the Hutterite colony. It's not known what
motivated Jakob to move in with the radical Hutterites, but one source describes it as a mission
to convince the Hutterites to adopt the more moderate Mennonite teachings. If this were the
intent, it evidently failed. A year later Jakob left the Hutterites and returned to Rosenberg,
unable to modify their views or come to terms with their practice of shunning community
members who broke church rules, including so-called "private sins."

My great-great-great-great-grandfather, Johann Bergthold, Daniel's third child, was thirteen when the family moved to Rosenberg. He probably received his early education back
in Harxheim as well but worked on the family farm in Rosenberg. He may have also worked
in the brick factory in Sczerecz. We know little of his life except that he married Katherine
Hubin, no doubt a childhood friend, whose family had immigrated with the Bergtholds from
the Palatinate. Johann and Katherine had three children, another Jakob, born in 1794, Marie,
and Daniel (these names were used by the family in almost every generation). They probably
lived in a house built near Grandpa Daniel's home and farmed the land with him. On Daniel's
death in 1806, the family moved into the patriarch's house, where they lived for many years.
Johann died in 1814 in Rosenberg at the age of forty-two.

Jakob Bergthold, the eldest son of Johann, grew up in Rosenberg, playing with the large
number of children in the village and hauling water for his mother from the well about fifty
yards from the house. He learned to farm at a young age by watching his father and grandfather plant and harvest their crops. In 1816 at the age of twenty-two, he married Elizabeth
Schrag. Jakob and Elizabeth were both born in Rosenberg and had no doubt played together
as children. They attended a few years of school together at the schoolhouse, which sat facing
the village common. Elizabeth may have attended school only long enough to learn to read the
Bible, because more education was thought wasteful for a girl.

As teenagers the young people would meet after church. According to Gerhard Lohrenz, "Boys would gather in one room and girls in another for part of the afternoon. Later everyone came together in the 'great room' to talk, sing and play games. Young couples who 'had an understanding' but were not officially engaged sat together. The young people were always well behaved."[34]

Jakob and Elizabeth's courtship and marriage followed the customs of the day. Lohrenz notes that when a young man wished to make a marriage proposal, he sought the help of the *Umbitter* (petitioner) who in turn visited the girl's parents. She was given the information and allowed a period of time to respond … It was the duty of the *Umbitter* to announce the engagement to the congregation when it had been finalized and to go house to house with a written wedding invitation.

Weddings were major social events for the entire village. "The village churches had no kitchens or fellowship halls for serving and dining. Therefore, most people were married at home, sometimes in the *Grootestow* (large room). More often than not, houses could not accommodate the whole village, so the barn would be cleaned of cobwebs and lined with tarpaulins. Every inch of the yard had to be swept and groomed, gardens weeded and trails through the gardens raked and sprinkled lightly with fine white sand. Benches were placed throughout the garden and yard to provide a place for guests to relax and visit."[35]

For his own wedding, Jakob wore a white shirt, black cravat, and a long coat like those worn by the minister. Elizabeth wore the black dress in which she had been baptized as an adult. But she had a white veil. Preparations for the wedding supper were going on in the summer kitchen. "The scent of baked ham and *Plumemoos* hung heavy over the house. Thickly sliced ham that had been baked to perfection and was dripping with sweet, syrupy sauce, baked potatoes in melted butter and garnished with green parsley, all the corn on the cob one could eat, *Zweiback* and seven kinds of sweet and sour pickles were on the menu. After the main course, there were *Apfelplats* and *Plummenplats* (apple and plum coffee cakes) and all kinds of *Klein Geback* (small baked delicacies). The *Tanten* (aunts) who served the tables would shake their heads in disbelief and amazement at the heaps of food the children could put away."[36]

Jakob, like his Grandfather Daniel, was an elected lay preacher, probably making his living as a farmer. By the 1800s, horses were widely used for farming, and single blade iron plows were in common use. Each farmer had several cows that were taken every day, together with the cows from each family, to a common grazing area.

During my visit to Rosenberg in 1997, I saw cows heading home in a line down the central lane in the village. As each cow reached the gate of its "family," it peeled off from the herd and entered the family compound without a signal from the cowherd.

Most of the farm production was used by the family and preserved for winter use by the women. The excess was taken to neighboring villages and to towns like Sczerecz to be traded for cloth and farm equipment.

Joseph Rohrer, a Catholic resident of Galicia, wrote in 1804:

Only a few Mennonite families remain in Galicia. They are honest, have little to do with ceremonials. They also speak some broken French (probably a holdover from the time the family spent in Alsace before moving to the Palatine), and their raising of cattle is the best in the land. Their dairying is exemplary, and their cheese, whose price is very cheap (because the Baptizer bargains as little as the genuine Moravian, but sets at once the cheapest price), is like the tastiest cheese that one can buy in the Swiss Alps. They are very temperate, keep themselves almost entirely from beer and brandy, and thus know how to bridle themselves. Rohrer goes on to say that in Rosenberg, where the Chief Magistrate was a Mennonite (perhaps a Bergthold), "Taxes are paid promptly, usually a little ahead of time; while in other places delinquencies have often occurred."[37]

As with many of the family moves, population growth, local politics, and sometimes internal conflicts among the settlers motivated emigration. I believe the Jakob Bergthold family left Rosenberg about 1820, because the records indicate that their third child, my great-great-great-grandfather, Daniel, was born in 1821 in Molotschna, several hundred kilometers to the south, as were their six younger children. Why did they move to Molotschna? Most likely the same reasons they had made so many moves before—for land, peace, and opportunity.

CHAPTER FIVE

THE MOLOTSCHNA OPPORTUNITY

The final years in Galicia must have been difficult for the Bergtholds. The population of the villages had increased rapidly due to continued immigration and large families, making it more difficult to find land to purchase at a reasonable price. Also, the area had changed from Austrian to Russian control, and the Czar revoked the law that had established freedom from military service. It's also possible that social and religious conflicts in the villages made them less attractive places in which to live. Rev. J.P. Linscheid wrote in 1933,[38] "Freedom from military service was revoked, and with it the settlers lost much of their customary way of life. Also, in the sphere of religion there was a tendency toward 'modernization.'" In addition, the work situation for the poorer among them was not favorable. This caused the "quiet ones in the land"[39] to look around for a home with more favorable conditions.

Whatever the reason, Jakob Bergthold and Elizabeth Schrag moved several hundred kilometers south to the larger and more prosperous German colonies near the Molotschna River in Central Ukraine. Although I found no definitive record, it's likely that Jakob and his family of two children (Jakob and Johan) moved to Alexanderthal, a Mennonite colony along the Dnieper River, around 1820 to join other Mennonite families they had known in Galicia, such as the Justs and Lidtkes. Descendants of these families, Phyllis and Virgil Lidtke and Roy Just and his wife, visited the Molotschna area in 1989. They described the area as follows:[40]

> My wife, Phyllis, and I, on our recent three-week trip to the Soviet Union in the summer of 1989, along with the Roy Justs, who instigated our tour, had the rare opportunity to travel to the Molotschna area of Ukraine. Our tour group was able to drive through numerous villages that remain—villages where our forefathers lived over a century ago. Today, however, they are occupied by native Russians; our German people have long since been scattered and driven from their homes.

Soon after arriving in Molotschna, Jakob and Elisabeth had their third child, Daniel (born in 1821), and later six additional children, for a total of nine. There's little in the record about their early lives in Molotschna, but they probably lived among many of the same people with whom they had grown up in Galicia.

In 1847, Great-Great-Grandfather Daniel married Katherine Linscheid in Molotschna. The Linscheid family had moved to Galicia from the Palatinate with the Bergtholds, and it's probable that the families moved to the Molotschna at the same time. Katherine's family had lived in a house very near the main well in Einsiedel, Galicia. As a child, she must have played and helped store potatoes and canned fruit in the same stone basement with an arched ceiling that I had visited in Ukraine in 1997. Near the ceiling of that basement, written in large letters carved in stone, I saw the words "Peter Linscheid—1827." Peter Linscheid was Katherine's father.

Gary in the basement of the Linscheid house in Einsiedel in 1997

Carved in stone in Linscheid basement—Peter Linscheid 1827

Unfortunately, the search for religious peace and civil freedom that prompted the move to Molotschna proved elusive once again. The Mennonites in the Molotschna colonies, like their counterparts throughout the region, were undergoing a period of intense change and conflict. In his book *The Molotschna Settlement*,[41] Heinrich Goerz described the situation encountered by the Bergtholds on their arrival to Alexanderthal. The original founders of the Molotschna settlement had come from the Danzig, Marienberg, and Ebing area in West Prussia. Their ancestors had emigrated from Holland some 250 years earlier because of religious persecution by the Spanish rulers who then governed the Netherlands. The first group of Molotschna settlers left Prussia in the summer of 1803, consisting of sixty-three families, many of whom had sold their farms at good prices. Between them they brought along ten thousand to twenty thousand gold ducats. "Their large canvas-upholstered wagons drawn by four or six horses were loaded down with fine furniture, chests, wardrobes, chairs, tables and bedsteads made of walnut wood. They were later followed by a large number of rather poor families who needed the support of their wealthier co-religionists."

The immigrants moved to their new settlement in Taurida province, on the left bank of the Molotschna River, which empties into the Sea of Azov. The land was granted them by the government of Russia along with financial inducements of interest-free loans for ten years to cover travel expenses and the purchase of horses, cattle, and lumber for building. The territory consisted of 320,000 acres of flat, fertile farmland. By the time the Bergtholds arrived in the 1820s, the Molotschna colonies had grown considerably in both size and prosperity. The total number of Prussian Mennonite families living in the colonies by the mid nineteenth century may well have been over one thousand.

By the 1860s, dozens of small villages had appeared along the Molotschna and its tributaries. Descriptions of these villages written at the time provide some clues about how the village of Alexanderthal must have looked when the Bergtholds arrived. The original buildings in the villages were improved during the administration of Johann Cornies. Cornies was a strong-willed leader of the Mennonites who was named "Deputy of all Mennonites" by the Russian government in 1817 at the age of twenty-eight. In 1830, he was appointed "Chairman for Life of the Society for the Advancement of Agriculture and Industry." Cornies played a major role in the economic and educational development of the Molotschna colonies. He ordered that farm buildings be erected in a uniform style. Everything on the farms had to be consistent. The wooden gables of the homes and fences were to be painted red and yellow. D.H. Epp wrote: "Woe to the German settler who did not paint his roadside fence in time. Cornies was able to sentence any culprit who did not comply into forced labor."[42] All houses in Molotschna had a similar layout. Most of the Molotschna Germans spoke a dialect called *Plautdeutsch*, or Low German, that originated in Holland and the neighboring areas of Germany. It is here that the Bergtholds probably picked up the use of Low German words that they continued to mix liberally with their ancestral High German, even after migrating to America in the twentieth century.

Most likely the Bergtholds were among the poor and landless migrants who arrived after the region had been thickly settled. They probably rented land on which to farm or perhaps worked for wages for more wealthy landowners.

Because of their conservative religious beliefs and the predominant views of the village in which they settled, I believe the Bergtholds may have belonged to an off-shoot of the Mennonite Church called the *Kleine Gemeinde* (little church). The *Kleine Gemeinde* had split off from the larger congregation (*Grosse Gemeinde*) because of religious differences. The *Kleine Gemeinde* believed in baptism by immersion and radical separation of church and state, and rejected the "worldly" lifestyle that prosperity had brought to many Mennonites. The differences in belief were reflected in different dress and personal style as well. The *Kleine Gemeinde* wore beards, dark and rough clothing, and lived as simply as possible. Unlike their neighbors with their red and yellow gables, the rebels painted their gables only in dark blue paint. The expression *kjleenjementsch* (small church-minded) was long used in Molotschna to denote something old fashioned and behind the times.

Daniel and Katherine (Linscheid) Bergthold had a total of six children. Their first, my great-grandfather, Heinrich, was born in Molotschna on April 5, 1848. Heinrich was educated in the schools of the Molotschna colony, which were much better than the schools back in Galicia. He must have shown an aptitude for speaking and a devotion to religion, because he later became a minister.

In addition to the religious conflicts that had appeared in the Molotschna colony, a social revolution was taking place that no doubt affected the Bergtholds greatly and motivated their move from Molotschna to the Kuban River. The core of the problem was the treatment of the landless, among which the Bergtholds were numbered. "Economic circumstances in Molotschna changed radically during the first 50 years of the settlement. In the early years, it was possible for any family of even the most modest means to settle down in the ever-increasing number of newly established villages and lay claim to a farmstead of 65 dessiatins."[43] However, all this changed with a rapid increase in population in Molotschna in the 1840s. The number of destitute and landless families kept increasing in the villages. This led to a great deal of dissatisfaction, quarrels, and general social unrest. Little by little, the community divided itself into two hostile camps: the landowners and the landless. The landowners made up less than a third of the population but had most of the votes in the village assemblies.

Meanwhile, religious bickering was also increasing among the Mennonites. The privileged began to drift away from the austere behavior and Evangelical beliefs of their ancestors to practice a more formalistic form of religion. The poor, who were more traditional, were not in agreement with these worldly trends. Six members of the Gnadenfeld Congregation of Molotschna, who disagreed with the trends in the established Church, met at a private home and celebrated communion without the presence of a minister. The established Mennonite Church was outraged by this heresy and ordered that the six be shunned by the community. This led to the formation of a new congregation, the Mennonite Brethren Church, founded officially on January 6, 1860. A document of secession was drawn up and signed by eighteen family heads. It was designed to guide the Church back to its origins: literal interpretation of the Holy Scriptures and strict adherence to the teachings of Menno Simons. The members of the newly formed Mennonite Brethren Church were primarily from the poor or even utterly indigent class within the Mennonite society.

I don't know exactly why the Bergtholds left the Molotschna for the Kuban colony, but around 1866, they and several other *Kleine Gemeinde* families moved two hundred kilometers east, past the Sea of Azov on the Kuban River. Heinrich was about eighteen years old at the time of the move.

CHAPTER SIX

THE KUBAN RIVER SETTLEMENT

The relationship between the old church and the Mennonite Brethren in Molotschna had not been resolved, and the Brethren applied for permission to move east to the Caucasus Mountains. The permission was granted. In 1868, sixty-seven families, including the Bergtholds, moved to the banks of the Kuban River, on the eastern side of the Sea of Azov. Land was leased to the new settlers by a Russian aristocrat by the name of Orbeliani for twenty-five kopeks per dessiatin. Relocation from Molotschna was accomplished by horse and wagon. The entire distance was about three hundred kilometers and was covered in ten to fifteen days. The Kuban settlers built primitive shelters called *zemlins* (sod huts) by digging shallow caves and covering the roofs with sod. Later, straw and reed thatch were used for roofs, and houses were built of clay and logs.

A visitor several years later wasn't impressed by the villages along the Kuban. "I had a very poor impression of the Kuban Colony. Along the streets were hedges of woven shrubs; homes were fashioned of clay bricks covered with straw or reeds."[44] The Kuban terrain was virgin prairie. The deep sod covering the earth was very difficult to plow. Land needed for gardening was broken first and then land was tilled for planting grain. The settlers were filled with hope when the grain reached unusual heights, but their hope was dashed as strong winds bent over the long stalks and heavy heads of wheat, nearly wiping out the entire crop.

The disappointments in farming were matched by continuing social and religious problems. The love, unity, and contentment the Brethren expected in their new home were not to be found. Johann Classen wrote to his wife during the summer of 1864:

> There are new trials which we must endure in the course of the present experience. In the midst of overwhelming tasks and deficiencies on all sides, one must be very heedful not to become unloving and to look only to one's own needs … that circumstances here are what they are, is not unexpected—indeed, things will get worse but eventually will take a turn for the better again. The hills of gold must first turn to copper, and we must learn to be content therewith before better times can return … It seems to me that (the spiritual) life in the Molotschna is superior to that prevalent in the Kuban. Here the disposition towards covetousness is tested since everyone is in a state of need … As yet I have encountered little joy here in the Kuban. Many folk are ill … nearly all … with but few exceptions. The people in the Old

Colony have been very prejudicial. It is well, however, to wait patiently; in due course, circumstances will again change.[45]

The Kuban settlement consisted of two adjacent villages. The northern village was named Alexanderfeld (later Alexandrodar) in honor of Tsar Alexander II. The southern village was named Wohldemfuerst. It was later renamed Velikokniazhesk in honor of the Caucasian Governor, Grand Duke Michael Nikolaivitch. Frederick Liesch, a resident of the Kuban settlement in the early 1900s, described the two villages as he remembered them as a child:

> My earliest recollections are, of course, based on childhood memories and family activities of my early youth in Russia. My parents, my grandmother, sisters and brothers form a big part of my fondest recollections. Our school, villages, river, and the old grist mill with its big waterwheel. The mysteries of the interior of the mill. My uncle David Schaak, the hunter. Uncle Martin, the 6'5" giant blacksmith. Uncle Ludwig the 6'4" athlete. All these were responsible or were in many ways forming and shaping my aspirations in my early youth.
>
> We lived close to the southern tip of Russia. The Mennonites at that time occupied two villages in this area. Ours by the name of Alexandrodar. The next one was actually connected to our village by houses on both sides of the main road. All the houses had big lots and beautiful gardens with fruit and ornamental trees.
>
> This part of Russia was not the Steppes, but it was prairie. The only forested area was along the river valley, mostly of the hardwood variety. The River Kuban was to the west of our village. To the east the land rose in terraces, the first one just 200 yards back of the main road going through the center of the village. Then it was flat for about two miles with another rise gently sloping for probably 200-300 feet. As we lived in villages, the farmland was all in plots, from 40 acres to 200 acres per plot depending on the size and wealth of each farmer. We were one of the smaller landowners, but by renting from retired farmers we had about an average operation.
>
> Our house was built of adobe brick which in that climate seemed to be quite long lasting. The roof was made of tile made out of clay and fired in an oven like brick or pottery. Anything made of lumber such as window frames had to be imported in the raw and was manufactured in the village. Besides having a plant for making furniture, the village had a big iron machine shop with big blasting ovens for milling ore and making cast iron machinery such as plows, wagons, and old style threshing machines.

To us youngsters it was quite a treat when we were taken by our teacher and an official of the plant on an inspection tour. To us this was more of an exploration tour as we managed to get lost, which gave us an opportunity to explore areas which were not well suited for public inspection.

Each village had its own school. Ours consisted of four classrooms, each accommodating between forty and fifty students, most of them not of the intellectual variety. I myself was not one of the brighter stars but still did quite well in bribes for helping others in geography and the three Rs. I should say two Rs as my writing was not called penmanship and has suffered deterioration over the years."[46]

The writer of this recollection, Frederick Liesch, had a brother named Gustav, who left the Kuban with him in the early 1900s to emigrate to Canada. Gustav's oldest child, Viola, was to marry a Bergthold by the name of Glenn many years later. Sadly, my parents, Glenn and Viola, died without learning that Viola's father and Glenn's grandfather had come to America from the very same settlement on the Kuban River in Southern Russia.

In one of the few conversations I had with my maternal grandfather, Gustav Liesch, about why his family left the Kuban some years after the Bergtholds, he shared with me that one of the driving forces in the move to America for his family was that life in the Kuban settlement was becoming increasingly dangerous. He told me stories about periodic raids by Caucasus tribesmen, who swept down from their homes in the mountains and robbed and occasionally killed the defenseless pacifist Mennonite farmers. Conflicts between pacifism and the strong need to defend themselves contributed to the move to America. It ultimately resulted in the weakening of the pacifist commitment, as illustrated by the enlistment in World War II by some of my uncles on the Bergthold and Liesch sides.

The decision to move to America from the Kuban by the Bergtholds was motivated more by the economic difficulties of living in the Kuban settlement and glowing letters describing the promised land of Minnesota from friends and relatives who had already left.

Six years after moving to the Kuban settlement in 1868, Heinrich Bergthold married Alvina Starke. The marriage was recorded in the city of Stavrapol, the Russian provincial capital city near the Kuban settlement. It's probable that the church marriage actually took place on the Kuban but was recorded in the capital. Alvina Starke had been born in Schoenlanka, Danzig, East Prussia on July 2, 1852. Only a few years after their marriage, Heinrich, age twenty-five, and Alvina, age twenty-four, took the bold move of emigrating to America in 1877 with their three small children—Katherina, Daniel, and Barbara—who had been born in the Kuban settlement.

The last cycle of Bergthold emigration in Europe took the family from Galicia, Southern Russia, and the Kuban to the Midwest of America and finally to California. Everywhere they went they were seen as modest, hardworking, devout people. The Mennonites were skilled, efficient farmers. This reputation also made it possible for them to find favor with kings and emperors, who hoped their skills and attitudes would influence their less productive neighbors.

CHAPTER SEVEN
GOING TO AMERICA

The trip to America was long and difficult, and it followed the same pattern of seeking and wandering by the family over several centuries. With money sent by previous immigrants and possibly the Mennonite Churches in America, Heinrich and Alvina traveled by train, boat, and wagon back to their ancestral land of Germany to the port of Bremen. There they boarded the ship *Westphalia* with other family members and old friends from the Kuban. The only things they carried with them were the homemade farm clothing and some farm implements from Russia.

Shortly after their arrival in New York and a difficult but brief quarantine on Ellis Island, the young family left by train to join earlier Mennonite immigrants in the State of Minnesota. The couple's next four children—Karolina, Heinrich, Johann, and Alvina—were born in Mountain Lake, Minnesota, the family's first home in the new country. The rolling hills of Minnesota, the warm summers and cold winters, must have reminded them very much of their former home in the Kuban. They were also comfortable living among Bergthold cousins who had immigrated about the same time and had also settled in the Mennonite farming villages of Mountain Lake and nearby Butterfield. Families such as the Linscheids and Ewys, among whom the Bergtholds had lived since the migration to the Palatinate and Galicia, also surrounded them.

The Mennonites in Minnesota were wheat farmers, their occupation in the Molotschna and Kuban as well. The Mennonite immigrants made a tremendous contribution to the economy of the American Midwest by bringing with them the wheat seed they had planted in the Ukraine and South Russia. This seed, called Turkey Red, doubled the previous harvests of wheat in America and was largely responsible for the rapid development of the wheat growing states in the late nineteenth century.

In June 1997, I visited Mountain Lake and Butterfield to look for evidence of the Bergthold family's sojourn in Minnesota. There I met Glen Linscheid, a descendant of the Galician Linscheids. Glen took me to visit an old barn between Mountain Lake and Butterfield, Minnesota. In the barn was a stone grave marker the farmer had hit with his plow on the crest of a hill on the farm. The name on the grave marker was John (Johann) Bergtholdt, Heinrich's son and elder brother of Jacob.

Gary with John Bergtholdt grave marker in Minnesota

Heinrich Bergthold was a farmer and lay preacher, much as many of my grandfathers had been before him. After living in Minnesota for a few years, Heinrich and Alvina and their seven children moved south to Lehigh, Kansas. Bachmann reports that the move was prompted by Alvina, who wanted to join her brothers and sisters in Lehigh. Heinrich soon regretted the move "as there is no good growth of grass, and hay is not fit for the cattle. It is coarse and hard because of the great heat, so the cattle go bad. And there is a shortage of water, on account of which all new immigrants have to go through yellow fever."[47]

Shortly after their arrival in Lehigh, Heinrich and Alvina's eighth child, my Grandfather Jacob ("Jake"), was born on November 4, 1885. After living in Kansas for a few years and adding two more children to the family, they moved on to Colorado, probably to serve a congregation of Mennonite Brethren who had set up a farming community in the area. Reverend Heinrich Bergthold was the minister in churches in Kirk and Jos, small towns east of Denver. He also farmed corn, a crop that depended on regular rain in the summer.

In 1939, Jake's son Victor visited Kirk, Colorado with a traveling musical quartet. There he found many people who remembered the Bergthold family, including a Mrs. Fast, who remembered Jake as a young boy. Mrs. Fast took Vic to see the farm where Jake was raised and the church where Henry preached. The church was made of one-by-twelve rough-sawed lumber. The school where Jake attended was a one-story building made of adobe. The Bergthold farmhouse was also made of adobe. The well was powered by a windmill and pumped only a small stream of water. The few corn stalks that were standing were withered and drooping. The woman who lived there said, "No rain and no crop this year." Vic imagined that this must have been the same condition that drove the family to move on to Texas.

We know that Heinrich and Alvina packed up their small children and went to Texas to farm for a time, only to be driven back to Lehigh, Kansas by floods and storms that ruined their crops and an outbreak of malaria that threatened their health.

In 1889 and again in 1893, the US government opened up large sections of fertile land for homesteading in the panhandle of Oklahoma. On September 16, 1893, Heinrich and his son Jacob, now a young boy of eight, and other close relatives, took part in the great land rush to the Cherokee Strip. Each "runner" claimed a quarter section of land near the town of Fairview. After making sure of their claim, they returned to Kansas to prepare for the move to their new home. Harry A. Martens, a relative of the Bergtholds who also took part in the land rush, later described the process of setting up the homestead. It was a pattern that had been repeated numerous times by the Bergtholds in Switzerland, the Palatinate, Galicia, Molotschna, Kuban, and Minnesota. Martens remembers:

> It was decided to return (to Oklahoma) by horse and wagon to construct a dwelling. They chose the Northeast corner of the farm as the site and dug down three feet, made a roof of cedar logs and long stem grass. This "dug out," as it was called, was about twelve by fourteen feet, but several months later it was enlarged to twelve by twenty feet. After working three weeks, they returned to Kansas to move the family. A railroad boxcar was loaded with furniture, farm implements and supplies and shipped to Enid, Oklahoma, forty miles from Fairview. Grandfather, grandmother and the girls rode on the train while the young boys drove a team of horses pulling a heavily loaded wagon. This trip, which took eight days, was not soon forgotten. Uncle Henry recalls how on the last night of the trip they were encamped along the

Eagle Chief Creek, ten miles Northwest of Fairview. These five boys, ranging in age from seven to nineteen, had heard much of the fierce Indians in the Oklahoma Territory. Fear gripped their hearts when, on this dark night, they heard hoof-beats and loud voices saying, "Let's string him up right here in this tree." However, upon peering out of their hiding place in the wagon they were relieved to see a group of cowboys butchering a deer which they had strung up in the tree. The family now numbered nine children and their parents. Financially they were poor, but happy and thankful to have a farm and a home of their own." [48]

Heinrich's son Jake Bergthold and his wife, Bertha, had been married on June 11, 1911 in Corn, Oklahoma. They settled a piece of land in Homestead, Oklahoma, where sons Emerson and Elwood were born. My father, Glenn, was born in Bessie, Oklahoma a year later. Evidently crops were poor during those early years in Oklahoma, because the family had to sell their land. In 1916, they moved to Fairview, Oklahoma, where Victor, Anna, and Louise were born. After moving to Fairview, Jake worked for the Longbell Lumber Company for a few years, until news from relatives who had found a new land of golden opportunity caused them to once again pick up their meager belongings to start a new life.

At this point in the Bergthold history, the family needed to move again to sustain their growing families and escape the lack of fertile land to support them. News of opportunity in California persuaded them that they could make a living there.

CHAPTER EIGHT

THE FINAL MOVE TO CALIFORNIA

The family, now including six children (including my father, Glenn), came to California by train and arrived in Shafter, where they were met by the Schapanskys. Aunt Louise Schapansky was not really Bertha's aunt, but she was called "Aunt" because she and her parents had raised Bertha as a little girl. Bertha's mother, Anna Schapansky Just, had died in childbirth.

The family probably stayed with the Schapanskys until they could find a place of their own. Victor remembers sitting on "Uncle" Schapansky's knee as a four-year-old child. Uncle Schapansky had the biggest hands Vic had ever seen. In his hand he held a huge orange, which he began to peel. Vic had never before eaten an orange. He gave Vic the small slices on the blossom end of the orange he called "kisses." It was the sweetest and most delicious thing Vic had ever tasted.

Vic also remembers the excitement of coming home from school and seeing several families from surrounding farms gathered for butchering day on the Bergthold farm. Butchering several huge hogs took two days, as it had hundreds of years before. Vic remembers stirring the *grieben* in the *meagrope* with a long wooden paddle and being told by his dad to never stop stirring because the little pieces would burn and ruin the entire batch. What a responsibility for a little boy! The chief butcher was Charlie Gloeckler, a rotund neighbor famous for his ability to stick pigs, make headcheese, and taste raw pork to make sure the seasoning for the sausage was just right.

John Bergthold remembered[49] that Jake and Bertha first rented the Altringer Farm in Shafter, California, where John was born in 1925. A year later the family moved a few miles to Wasco, where Jake rented a forty-acre farm from Mr. Rapp. John remembers that a landing field for airplanes was located at the back of the property, and John and his brothers would spend many hours watching the small airplanes land and take off. Apparently, the Bergtholds moved several times during those years, always renting their farmland. Finally, in 1939–40, they had a profitable year (cotton prices were high due to the coming war), and they could afford to buy a farm. They put a down payment on a twenty-acre place on Kimberlina Avenue south of Wasco, California, and my Uncle Marty remembers that Jake purchased a two-bedroom house from Henry Vogt, a nearby farmer, and moved it to the new farm. On this farm they grew alfalfa, corn, onions, potatoes, watermelon and cucumbers.

The family had a huge garden behind the house, just like the houses in the Palatinate, Galicia, and Molotschna. They grew most everything they needed in the garden and traded garden produce and farm animals for staples such as flour and sugar. They traded at the Villegas Country Store for one-hundred-pound sacks of flour and other things they needed but couldn't grow. Marty remembers that Jake was obsessed with weeds and would make the boys work daily to weed out any weeds in their garden and even the weeds that grew along the road of their neighbors. Jake and the boys farmed the twenty acres with a team of mules, because Jake felt that he could get more out of his acreage with mules than with tractors. Their crops were mainly sorghum, potatoes, and cotton.

Delphine, John, and Martin had been born in Shafter, and Daniel, Dorothy, and James were born in Wasco. Jake and Bertha raised thirteen children and lost their fourteenth child named Beatrice, in childbirth. Nevertheless, the house was always full of children and laughter. The family had little money, but they always had lots of love and good food.

after mom's funeral apr 2, 1953

The thirteen Jake and Bertha Bergthold children: my father, Glenn, is fourth from left

Grandpa Jake had a smokehouse where he smoked the hams and bacon from the family pigs. Straw and corncobs were used to make the smoke in a little pit, and the smoke would travel up a ten-foot tunnel from the pit to the smokehouse. Jake would stay up all night to keep the fire going. The bacon made the best biscuits and gravy anyone has ever tasted.

The Bergthold kids learned how to work from a very young age. The boys would work in the garden as young children and then hire out to neighbors when they reached the age of ten or eleven. Jake always expected them to contribute half their earnings to the family coffer. The four firstborn boys were the happiest boys in town, according to Vic, when the next four children born in the family were girls. This was because the girls took over the inside chores such as cooking and washing dishes. Vic remembers the girls washing dishes while standing on chairs to reach the sink and churning butter on a churn that was taller than they were.

There were very few toys and no luxuries during the Depression years. Poverty was softened by humor and shared with friends and neighbors. A favorite game of the boys was "saw me," in which they would hide behind the banks of the reservoir and pop up their heads to see if anyone else was looking. If they saw another pair of eyes, they would raise a middle finger in the air and yell "saw me." Perhaps the humor came from the use of the forbidden obscene gesture.

Grandma Bertha's work never ended, but she was ever jolly and was never heard to complain about her difficult life. Vic says she was quite subdued but smiled all the time and was quick to laugh. She was known as a great cook, and her fried chicken was wonderful. Bertha's huge pantry just off the kitchen was always loaded with jars of home-canned fruit, pickles, and freshly made *zwieback*. The aroma of those small round buns filled the house with a smell of love and security. My earliest memories include the yeasty smell of those fresh-backed *zwieback* pulling me like a magnet to the walk-in pantry. High on a shelf, far from the reach of a tip-toed little boy, I could see the steam still rising from the golden two-tiered buns. With pathetic eyes, I could entice my grandmother to take down a *zwieback,* tear off the little top bun and smear it with freshly-made butter. My father also remembers taking lunch to school with sandwiches of home-made bread smeared with *grieben-schmaltz,* which was pork lard. The "English kids" would eagerly trade their baloney sandwiches for this Mennonite culinary delight.

Grandpa Jake on Kinsley St. in Santa Cruz, California

Grandpa Jake was efficient, thrifty and devout. He always said his prayers in High German, which only the oldest children understood. Although Jake and Bertha spoke English and Low

German, they felt the language of God was High German. According to Vic, Jake had quite a temper. If one of the kids misbehaved at the table, he would simply point at the door and out the kid would go without a question. When they moved to Santa Cruz, Jake was frustrated that the cantelopes and watermelons did not thrive in the foggy weather, but he enjoyed his huge tomato plants and prolific fruit trees. He also raised chickens in spotlessly clean chicken coops. On Sunday morning, he would walk to the back of his lot and return with a white hen in each of his hands, dangling from the neck. As he neared the back lawn, he would twirl them and with a quick snap of his wrist, the hens would fly to the ground and do their last headless dance. An hour later the hens would be in a pot boiling with noodles Grandma had just made and cut by hand. No meal was ever fresher or made with more love.

Christmas was a time of great joy and feasting, as it had been throughout the Bergthold history. As was the custom in Galicia, each child would receive a bag of candy and nuts after the Christmas Eve church service. Since coming to California, a precious and rare treat was added to each bag: a juicy California orange. These Christmas oranges were often hoarded and hidden from the young brothers and sisters. The last one to eat his orange would slurp it with exaggerated delight to maximize the jealousy and annoyance felt by all. In addition, there was often a pair of socks included in the stocking, which would elicit great whoops of laughter as the children would yell "fin fein fimt," their version of German "fifteen cents."

My maternal grandfather Gustav Liesch in Bakersfield, California

My own parents Glenn and Viola never knew that the Lieschs and Bergtholds lived in the same village in the Kuban, but they shared the same cultural and religious traditions. Glenn and Viola met when she heard him singing at a Mennonite conference event. She fell in love with his smile and the rest is certainly history. Both of their families were active in the Mennonite Brethren Church in Central California. Their early marriage in Lost Hills and Wasco was full of love but a struggle financially. I remember my mother saying she put wet towels around my infant crib to protect me from the intense heat of the Valley, because of course there was no air conditioning. My dad worked in the oil fields but eventually his love of music led him to Bakersfield to work as a manager in Tracy's Music Store. When Tracy died, my dad was able to build a business of his own, Glenn's Music Store, where he sold guitars, records and sheet music, while my mom worked alongside him keeping the books. Bakersfield was known as the "Nashville of the West" in those days, and my dad sold many guitars to musicians like Buck Owens and Merle Haggard and sometimes had to repossess them when the purchasers couldn't make the payments. My youngest brother Jack and his wife took over the store when my dad retired.

My parents Glenn and Viola in the early years in Central California

One of the moments I remember in my early years in Wasco was a day when I returned from elementary school and told my mother that I had heard the other kids talk derogatorily about "Okies." My mother took my face in her hands and said solemnly, "Gary, did you know your father is an Okie?" I was stunned. I had no idea he had been born in Bessie, Oklahoma. It had a significant impact on me as a young boy, as I learned not to judge people by their ethnic or racial origin. I was the son of an Okie and I had better be proud of it.

My mother Viola with myself and my brother Roger in Wasco

My younger brothers and I benefited from the stability of a family that no longer needed to move because the crops failed or the government demanded military service. By the time my youngest brother Jack was born in 1947, the family was better off financially, but the pacifist values remained and re-emerged when Jack applied for and received a conscientious objector exemption from the draft during the Viet Nam war years later. We were proud of him.

While most of my Bergthold uncles and aunts knew relatively little of the early history of their family, perhaps the painful memories of the old country were best forgotten as the family worked to become true Americans. The youngsters knew vaguely that they were "German" but had no knowledge of their beginnings in Switzerland and the travels of their grandfathers and grandmothers in Galicia, Ukraine, and Russia. But there were reminders. Their favorite family foods were still *varenike* and *borscht*, Ukrainian words. The watermelon they enjoyed with *rollkuchen* was still called *arabus*, a Russian word.

A poem written by a German-Russian immigrant describes the process of assimilation and forgetting:

THE GREAT FORGETTING

BY SOPHIA BRENNEISEN

A child can't return inside its mother,
Nor us back to South Russia, where we
Wandered from in the year of our Lord 1886,
Me and my husband, Hannes, looking for a
Better life in Dakota.

We stayed through hunger. We sprinkled seeds
On gunny sacks, and cooked sparrows
That caught themselves scratching there.

We stayed through prairie fires. At night
The whole world looked like it was burning.

We stayed through cold and blizzards. We
Ate flour one winter. Just flour. We cried
Out: "Ach, lieber Gott, erbarm dich doch

Uber unsere Not—'Have pity on us for our needs.'"
We worked and prayed our way through
All those bad times. Our children were too young to
Remember.

We let them think theirs was the only world
That had ever been. Of snowplows and lights
And tractors, of thick sandwiches and heavy stews.

Things got better. We covered the dirt floor
With boards, then those with linoleum,
And in our last years, that linoleum with carpeting.

We carpeted everything, wall to wall. Our grown
Children visited. "You even put carpet around the
Toilet in the indoor bathroom," they said.

We suffered their scolding in silence,
Wanting nothing of those early years
But to forget.[50]

I have traveled to Ukraine four times. During my visits, I have been asked by many Ukrainians why the United States is so generous in providing technical assistance and financial aid for rebuilding the healthcare system and for building private business and social organizations. I know there are large geo-political reasons for this generosity, particularly in light of the recent war of aggression by Russia, but I answered in a much more personal way when I spoke to the school children in Sczercezc in the late 1990s:

You gave our grandparents a home when they needed one and you shared your food and culture with us. Millions of Americans trace their roots through Ukraine. You also gave us the Turkey Red wheat seeds that made our Midwest rich. We are now simply repaying a debt that we have long owed.

CHAPTER NINE

PUTTING DOWN MY OWN ROOTS

The rich history of the Bergthold and Liesch families didn't end with the migration to California. Many of the same customs and traditions were prevalent in the lives of my parents, grandfathers Jake and Gus, and their hard-working and loving wives. The butchering of animals, the creation of gardens, the cooking of special foods, were all carried from generation to generation.

My wife, Linda, whose father, Arvid Carlson, immigrated from Sweden to Ellis Island and California in the early 1900s, and whose grandparents on her mother Linnea's side also had families that had immigrated from Sweden, carried forward the same respect for traditions such as *Julotta*—the Christmas Eve celebration, Santa Lucia Day in December, *korv* sausage, Swedish pancakes, meatballs, and fragrant saffron buns.

It should be no surprise that Linda and I continued the traditions of food and travel in our own lives. We traveled not from desperation or persecution but in search of new adventures and opportunities. In our early twenties, barely out of college, we took a great leap and sent in an application to join the Peace Corps in 1962, a program that had just started under President John F. Kennedy.

Peace Corps Volunteers Greeting JFK on the lawn of the White House, 1962; photo by Gary

To our astonishment, we were accepted, and within weeks we had sold our belongings (no *meagrope* to bring) and took our first plane rides to Washington D.C. for training and ultimately to Addis Ababa, Ethiopia to teach.

Gary and Linda in Addis Ababa, Ethiopia 1962

Gary with his students in Addis Ababa

Linda reading to neighbor Yohannes in Addis Ababa

Those years in Africa were formative in our lives, because after our two-year tour of duty, we then traveled back to Washington D.C. for a year while I worked in the office of the Peace Corps psychiatrist Dr. Joseph T. English, and Linda taught in a high school in the heart of D.C. This international experience propelled me into a lifetime of work and travel in over forty different countries around the world.

In 1969, from Washington D.C. to Boston, we picked up our belongings again so that I could enroll in a Ph.D. program in Human Development at Harvard University and manage Peace Corps recruiting in the region. My Ph.D. dissertation was an evaluation of the impact of the Peace Corps on Ethiopian students, and we spent six months back in Ethiopia (with infant daughter Lara) while I did my research. Back to Boston where Linda taught at Brookline High School, and Eric was born, before our next emigration began in 1970—to Quito, Ecuador, where I took a position with USAID as a Social Science Advisor to the Ministry of Education.

Ecuador also offered us the opportunity to add a most beloved member to our family, Nicolas Alejandro ("Alex"), whom we adopted from the Aldea del Ninos orphanage outside of Quito before we made our next move—to Managua, Nicaragua, where I taught at a management school called Instituto Centroamericano de Administracion de Empresas (INCAE).

In 1974, after two years in Nicaragua, we returned to California for our last big move to settle down in Santa Cruz, California, for the next forty years. The move to Santa Cruz proved to be a way to incorporate all the family traditions and lifestyle that had been so important in shaping our lives. It was also a place where my grandparents had visited on vacation and lived in their retirement years, and Linda's and my parents were located there too.

Gary, Eric, and Alex at the Aldea del Ninos outside of Quito, Ecuador

The kids in Nicaragua

Finding the house on Paul Sweet Road in Santa Cruz made it possible to live out my dream of being a "gentleman farmer." The small two-line advertisement in the newspaper was cryptic, and the owner of the house seemed to try to keep us from seeing it: "There's a dirt road," she said. Fine by us, we thought. Driving down that dirt road the next day, the smell of eucalyptus brought strong memories of Ecuador, and as we entered the valley where the house was located, we both gasped. It was our own *klushof*—a long, green, three-sided valley with steep sides and even a few grapevines planted by priests of the nearby monastery.

The house itself wasn't fancy. There was little vegetation around it, but there was a fence, a barn, and space for a good garden. The kids could walk to the elementary school without crossing a street. It was an easy decision for us. The house with its surrounding acreage was just what we wanted.

The house on Paul Sweet in 1975

In Santa Cruz, we were able to recreate many of the traditions our families had brought with them to America: the gardening, raising of animals (we had pigs, chickens, a lamb, a steer, and various ponies, horses, donkeys, and dogs), and the making of family favorites like sausage and sauerkraut. We butchered several pigs with the help of family and expert retired butchers, roasted goats with the help of workers from Oaxaca, and my brother Jack helped us build a summer kitchen with a wood oven that produced Thanksgiving turkey and many pizzas for our friends.

The original barn and garden area on Paul Sweet Road

The garden area after Gary tilled it

"Garden of 'Eatin'"—idea for the garden sign came from Grandpa Jake,
a reference to the Biblical "Garden of Eden"

The garden produced quantities of vegetables

With grandson Eli in the Santa Cruz garden

In between my trips around the world training physicians and evaluating health programs, I spent my free time helping Linda with her Ph.D. studies at the University of California, Santa Cruz and San Francisco. She had supported me in my travels, and now was the time to support her to achieve her goals. She received her Ph.D. in 1985 and did her own traveling from Santa Cruz to San Francisco, Washington D.C., and around the country with her health policy work.

The one thing that united us all in those years in Santa Cruz was that the whole family participated in the garden next to our house, just like my ancestors had over the years. The soil was rich from the manure of our many farm animals, although our kids shoveled it somewhat reluctantly and under duress. The kids painted the garden fences to atone for various offenses, but the reward was the taste of corn picked and eaten within fifteen minutes, fresh eggs from our chickens, and all manner of pork raised and often butchered in the barn.

Preparing the fire to smoke the sausages with our donkey in the background

Smoking the sausage in the traditional way

Making sausage on our deck

Linda stirring pig fat and making lard and grieben in a meagrope

I longed for Emmenthal cows, but while we lived in the "country," there wasn't enough land to support a real herd of any kind. So my brother Roger created these substitutes, which the deer or coyotes sometimes knocked down in their effort to test whether they were real.

Gary and Roger with "Emmenthal" cows

With grandsons Jacob and Eli on a tractor

I had several tractors in Santa Cruz. My favorite was a John Deere L 1938, the year of my birth. There was another more modern tractor that pulled a wagon in which I could haul the kids around the valley. I also had a manure spreader, which I used to take neighbor kids on rides up and down the road. When we finally left Santa Cruz in 2014, my biggest regret was giving up my tractors and my huge and productive garden. What had been fun and easy in my younger years was now becoming more difficult to maintain.

The 1938 John Deere L

Our children grew and thrived in Santa Cruz, learning to take care of and feed animals, grow vegetables, slide down the hillside on cardboard, and contribute to family life on our little farm.

Eric, Lara, and Alex (and one of our dogs named "Dusty") in Santa Cruz in late 1970s

Our family in Santa Cruz around 1985

My brother Jack took great interest in keeping Mennonite food traditions alive in our family, and helped with butchering and cooking. He taught Lara how to make *zwieback* and during the years he lived in Santa Cruz, he participated in many opportunities to share some of the best family recipes.

My brother Jack with our daughter Lara making zwieback

During the years in Santa Cruz, Linda and I had the joy of watching our three children—Lara, Eric, and Alex—grow into loving and productive adults. We added a wonderful member to our family in 1996 when Eric met and married Ali Kincaid after both had been in the Peace Corps in Eritrea.

Ali and Eric Bergthold in Eritrea in 1996

Over the next years, we welcomed four grandchildren whom we love and admire to the Bergthold clan: Kincaid, Jacob, Charley, and Eli. We celebrated special anniversaries together in 2021 for our sixtieth wedding anniversary and Linda's eightieth birthday.

Gary and Linda with the four grandchildren in 2021

Our family in 2021 at Laguna Beach, California for Gary and Linda's
Sixtieth Wedding Anniversary and Linda's Eightieth Birthday

Before I began studying the history of my family, I thought of my ancestors as lifeless relics of a distant past, like the bones of saints on display in dark catacombs. However, by traveling to their places, walking on their streets, and sitting in their homes, I no longer see them as disconnected from my life. Their historical context parallels ours in many ways:

- We and they have experienced the hatred and violence across religious and ethnic divides that forced them to flee comfortable lives and that continue to affect our world;

- Rapid technological change from the printing press to the threshing machine to the Internet have both enriched our lives and caused deep disruption;

- Threats of worldwide epidemics from the black plague to influenza to COVID-19 have caused widespread fear and uncertainty; and,

- Terrorism from the Swiss Inquisition's burning stakes to our September 11th assault have caused profound changes in our daily lives.

We have all reacted to adversity in different ways. Sometimes we flee. Sometimes we stay and fight in different ways. Bergtholds are wanderers and seekers and always have been. We've moved for many reasons, but always in search of a better life and more opportunity. We work hard. We value family, food, and community. We laugh at adversity. We are Bergtholds.

As Thornton Wilder ends his book *The Bridge of San Luis Rey:*[51]

There is a land of the living and a land of the dead, and the bridge is love, the only survival, the only meaning.

ENDNOTES

1   I owe a great deal to the many helpful individuals and sources I found as I attempted to clarify the puzzles in the Bergthold historical record. First, I want to credit my wife, Linda, who helped me organize and edit all the information I located. She found *FriesenPress* and helped me put together the final manuscript. My cousin Roland Bergthold was also instrumental in my journey, and I would not have succeeded without his encouragement and input and the work he did on the Roland Bergthold family genealogy. Through the Internet I also met and later visited Glen Linscheid of Butterfield, Minnesota, whose family were Bergthold relatives. Glen had researched the Galician Mennonite history and generously shared with me his substantial knowledge and sources. Without the help of Dr. Andrew Tuziak, my guide and translator, I would not have been able to interview Mr. Vogt, who provided definitive links to the Mennonites who lived in the villages. Andrew continued to guide later visitors to the area.

Many other people helped me as well. I found and joined an organization on the Internet called the *American Historical Society of Germans from Russia,* which had amassed an enormous amount of information about the Mennonite immigrants to Ukraine and Russia. Through the AHSGR I met Doris Dahl Mizell, a Bergthold cousin who had researched her family genealogy, including the Bergthold line, to its earliest known members. Just a week before preparing for a trip to Ukraine, I posted a notice in a Mennonite chat room on the Internet telling about my trip and plan to visit the ancestral villages. The next day I received two replies from people who not only knew the German names for these places but also had themselves visited the villages within the past year. Another major source of family history has been Patricia Ross Hubin Myren and Nina Ross Myren Schroepfer, *Radicals to Realists: A Mennonite Legacy, from the Ancestors of Katherine Bergthold and Peter Hubin to Their Descendants, Beginning in 1525.*

2   Peter Bachmann, *Mennoniten en Kleinpollen.* Compiled from Peter Bachmann, Professor at the Staatsgymnasium, Kolomyja, Translated by Charles M. Anderson, 2000. Published privately. Bachmann writes: "These had been traumatic years in Europe. Religious persecution of the Protestants, numerous wars including the Thirty Years' War of Westphalia, and rapid population growth, created strong pressures causing many to leave their homes in search of peace. The immigrant movement started in the peasant heartland of Europe. Ponderously balanced in a solid equilibrium for centuries, the old structures began to crumble at the opening of the modern era. One by one, rude shocks weakened

the foundations until some climactic blow suddenly tumbled the whole into ruins. The mighty collapse left without homes millions of helpless, bewildered people. These were the army of immigrants."

3   Private correspondence from Berchtold Moser. June 2000; and T P Miller a.k.a. Emil E Ewy 21 April 1998, a compilation, p.1.

4   Hanspeter Jecker, *The Sanctified Rebel Heretics (Ketzer-Rebellen-Heilige)*, Liestal, *Switzerland. 1998.* Jecker is a Professor of Historical Theology and Ethics at the Theological Seminary Bienberg in Switzerland and was a very helpful source for much of the information about Berchtold/Bergthold history. Jecker notes that the earliest mention of the name Berchtold dates to a 1569 church book from Sissach when a Peter Berchtold of Thurnen functioned as a godfather at two baptisms of the sons of couples who wanted to be "with the true Christ." This was a way of describing Anabaptists. Another important source for the Anabaptists was the research done by Richard W. Davis that I found on this unsecured website: mennosearch.com and in email correspondence with Davis.

5   The Mennonite Library and Archives at Bethel College in North Newton, Kansas published *Index to Mennonite Immigrants on United States Passenger Lists 1872–1904* in 1986. The book was compiled and edited by David A. Haury.

6   To find out more about the various spellings of the name Bergthold, I researched an Internet site on the name Bartold/Berthold https://bartold.com/genealogy/index.html and was able to trace the name through various historical periods going way back to Berthold I (The Bearded 1024–1078), the first Duke of Zahringer. His second son, Berthold II, continued the Zahringer line. Berthold IV had a long and prosperous reign and built several major castles, including Neuenburg (~1175) and Fribourg (1157). His son, Berthold V, greatly expanded the Zahringer lands in modern-day Switzerland and is credited with founding both Bern and Thun. Today it's possible to see remnants of that period. The statue at Freiburg's (Fribourg) Bertoldsbrunnen (Bertold's Fountain) depicts the "Reitersiegel" (mounted victory statue) of Bertold II of 1187. In Fribourg, there is a major bridge named after them. Bern also has statues and Brunnensaule commemorating them.

7   Jacob Bergthold (b. c1709) was also known as Johann Jacob Bergthold. It was the Swiss and German custom to be called by the second name. For example, if you were named Hans Ulrich Bergthold, you would be called Ulrich or Uli. If your wife was named Anna Maria, she would be called Maria. Johann Jacob Bergthold would also be known as Jacob Bergthold. It was common to have two brothers called Jacob when one was named Jacob and the other Johann Jacob. The names Jacob and Daniel are prevalent in all of our history. (Source: Richard W. Davis, private correspondence, 2003).

8   Through Jean Jacques and a woman named Beth Bergdolt Parker, I learned that there are many links between our branch of the family and other branches. I put Beth and Jean-Jacques together in order to find our (possibly) mutual lineage in the Berchtolds of Switzerland.

9   Conversation with Tony in Thurnen, 2000.

10 Documents shared with me by Veronica Kollreuter of the Klushof. Some information found in the Jecker book, op.cit.

11 See website of the Klushof. Unsecured. www.klushof.ch

12 Ibid.

13 Jecker op.cit.

14 Information about the sale of the Klushof can be found at Staatsarchiv Basel-Landschaft (StABL) in Liestal, AA Urkunden Nr.968.

15 The Bauernkrieg of 1653 was a peasant revolt in search of fiscal relief from the authorities. Although it was quelled and many participants executed, some of their demands were later met. See in Wikipedia https://en.wikipedia.org/wiki/Swiss_peasant_war_of_1653

16 Jecker op.cit.

17 Ibid.

18 Email exchange with Hanspeter Jecker, November 26, 2003. Additional information in this section about Alsace is also validated by Rebecca McCoy in "Religious Accommodation and Political Authority in an Alsatian Community, 1648-1715." *Journal of Ecclesiastical History,* Vol. 52, No.2, April 2001.

19 Adam Giesinger, "From Catherine to Krushchev." *AHSGR,* 1981.

20 See the Mennonite Encyclopedia https://gameo.org/index.php?title=Welcome_to_GAME

21 According to the genealogist Richard W. Davis at mennosearch.com (and private email correspondence to me March 13, 2003), Daniel was born at Schifferstadt, but his father, Johann Jacob, died at Assenheim. Assenheim and Schifferstadt were part of the same Mennonite congregation, and he may have lived at Schifferstadt for a while and then apparently moved to nearby Assenheim after the birth of Daniel.

22 From Richard W. Davis, it is likely that Daniel Bergthold (b. c1747) was the son of Johann Jacob (b. c1709), who was probably the son of Freidrich Berchthold (b. c1679), who was probably the son of Fridli (which is a form of Friedrich) (b. c1636), who was the son of Peter Berchthold (b. c1605), who was the son of either Hans or Melchior

Berchthold. In 1769, Daniel, Jakob's eldest son, acquired a plot of land and, with his father-in-law, operated a vinegar distillery. Margarete (Marie) Lichti, Daniel's wife, was the daughter of Jacob Lichti, a miller in Harxheim.

23   Bachmann, op.cit.

24   Ibid.

25   A *meagrope* was an essential part of the household equipment. The word means "bricked kettle," as it was bricked into a corner of the summer kitchen. It had a small door in front, which closed off the fire box. Here water was heated on wash days, and often clothes were boiled right in it. During butchering days, hogs were scalded in it and lard was rendered and ribs fried. When the frugal housewife had a large enough amount of fat or tallow, she used the *meagrope* to make white soap.

26   Janet Chase, "Golden Memories, The Kullman and Ricker Families."

27   Bachmann op.cit.

28   Myren and Schroepfer, op.cit.

29   Bachmann op.cit.

30   Ibid. The map is also displayed in an edited version of Bachmann's work, *We Did Take Root - 1881- Galicia to America – 1982,* p. 24.

31   Poem quoted from Bachmann, op.cit., p.165. Portions edited by Gary Bergthold. Also noted in Myren and Schroepfer, p. 62.

32   The Mennonite Encyclopedia, https://gameo.org/index.php?title=Bergthold,_Jakob_ (1766-1821).

33   Jerold A. Stahly, "Joseph and Elisabeth Mundlein, Amish Mennonite Leaders in Galicia and Poland," *Mennonite Family History,* January, 1990.

34   Norma Jost Voth, Mennonite foods and folkways from South *Russia: vol. 1.* Intercourse, Pa.: Good Books, 1990. p. 480. EMC, FRESNO, MHL, MLA.

35   Ibid.

36   Mary Francis, quoted in Voth.

37   Voth op.cit.

38 J.P. Linscheid, "Historical Review in remembrance of a Group of Mennonites Who Emigrated in 1883 from Galicia, Austria," translated from the original German by Harold W. Linscheid.

39 The term "quiet ones in the land" may have come from Psalms 35:20.https://www.kingjamesbibleonline.org/Psalms-35-20/. It is also noted in J.P. Linscheid, op.cit.

40 Personal memories from the Lidtkes.

41 I was not able to visit the Molotschna or Kuban Settlement areas in person for my research, so I have relied on resources including: Heinrich Goerz, *The Molotschna Settlement*, 1993, p.4; D.H. Epp, *Johann Cornies* – Epp's book available on Amazon; C.P. Toews, Heinrich Friesen, Arnold Dyck, *The Kuban Settlement*, Echo Historical Series, translated from the German by Herbert Giesbrecht, CMBC Publications, Winnipeg, Manitoba, 1989; C. Henry Smith, *The Coming of the Russian Mennonites, An Episode in the Settling of the Last Frontier 1874-1884*, Mennonite Book Concern, Berne, Indiana, 1927; Gerhard Lohrenz, *Heritage Remembered, A pictorial survey of Mennonites in Prussia and Russia*, CMBC Publications, Winnipeg, Manitoba, n.d.; Mary M.Enns, Mia: *The Story of a Remarkable Woman*, Christian Press, Winnipeg, Manitoba, n.d.; and Theodore C. Wenzlaff, *The Founding of the German Colonies in Russia*, FEEFHS Journal Volume VIII, n.d.

42 D.H. Epp, op.cit.

43 Ibid. One dessiatin was equal to 2.07 English acres.

44 Letters obtained from Frederick Liesch family.

45 See resources in Endnote #41.

46 Letters from Liesch, op.cit.

47 Bachmann, op.cit.

48 Letters obtained from Harry Martens in "Record of the Family of Peter P. Martens, 1844-1902 and Maria Bergthold Martens, 1853-1926."

49 John Bergthold, "John Henry Bergthold's Life Story" (distributed by the family at John's funeral in July 1997). Insights about the daily life in Wasco and later in Santa Cruz were shared in an article that Martin Bergthold wrote for the *2000 California Mennonite Historical Society*.

50 This poem *"The Great Forgetting"* (Sophia Brenneisen, a pseudonym used by author Ron Vossler) was published in the *American Historical Society of Germans from Russia Journal*, Spring 1997. Note: AHSGR has given me permission to use this poem since

they had no specific contract or agreement with the author, Ron Vossler, to restrict its use. The AHSGR also published my article on Galicia and Mr. Vogt in Gary Bergthold, "Explorations in Galicia," *AHSGR,* Summer 1998, Vol.21, No.2, pp.11-15.

51   Thornton Wilder, *The Bridge of San Luis Rey,* https://en.wikipedia.org/wiki/The_Bridge_of_San_Luis_Rey